This Holyes

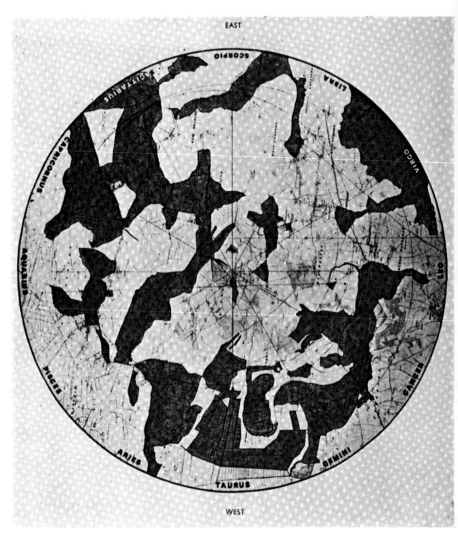

The Glastonbury Zodiac.
The effigies correspond with the styles of their respective celestial constellations.

This
HOLYEST
ERTHE

THE GLASTONBURY ZODIAC
AND
KING ARTHUR'S CAMELOT

BY

Oliver L. Reiser

HERMETICA

San Rafael, Ca

© Hermetica Press, 2007
First edition, Perennial Books, 1974

For information, address:
Hermetica Press, P.O. Box 151011
San Rafael, California 94915, USA

Library of Congress Cataloging-in-Publication Data

Reiser, Oliver Leslie, 1895–1974.
This holyest erthe, the Glastonbury zodiac and
King Arthur's Camelot / Oliver L. Reiser. — Reprint ed.
p. cm.
Includes bibliographical references.
ISBN-13: 978-1-59731-201-1 (pbk.: alk. paper)
1. Glastonbury (England)—Miscellanea. 2. Arthur, King.
3. Legends—England—Glastonbury. 4. Britons—Kings and
rulers—Folklore. 5. Great Britain—History—To 1066.
6. Camelot (Legendary place) 7. Arthurian romances—Sources.
8. Zodiac. I. Title.
DA690.G45R44 2007
936.2'383—dc22   2007027045

TO THE MEMORY OF
CHARLES H. BABCOCK

Contents

List of Illustrations

List of Plates

Foreword

This small volume was planned originally as a chapter in a larger book which is designed to present a more complete philosophy of history. But as the research and writing progressed, it became evident that the resulting body of materials on the Glastonbury Zodiac would become so substantial that a separate treatment must be provided. The larger enterprise is still under way. When completed, it will consist of other—earlier and later—episodes in our broad panorama of the "magnetic moments in human history." The Glastonbury saga, as it may be termed, has a thrust and a unity of its own which is deserving of separate treatment.

In the writing of this book I have had the assistance of a number of individuals. In England, Mr. John G. Bennett, Mrs. Marjorie von Harten, and Mrs. Mary Caine have provided me with much helpful discussion of relevant materials—some of this the product of their own research concerning the Somerset Zodiac and related matters. This is true also of other members of the "London Group," especially Miss Elizabeth Leader and Mrs. Janette Jackson. And on the American continent, several friends in Canada have assisted me with factual information and interpretations of data. My heaviest indebtedness is to the late Miss Blodwen Davies, with whom I have collaborated on other occasions. Also Mrs. Mary E. Allan of Vancouver, British Columbia, has been most helpful in several ways. As a resident of the area of the Maltwood Museum and as the friend of the late Mr. John A. Maltwood, she has been in a fortunate position to check on various questions. The search for the answers took her to the "Bible Box" at the Museum. I am grateful to her for arranging my visit to the Maltwood Museum and the conference with Mr. and Mrs. J. G. Austin, who at that time served as the curators of the Museum. It is also a pleasure to extend my thanks to Professor Mark Braham of Sir George Williams University, Montreal, for his many fruitful suggestions concerning the meaning of what we term the "Maltwood Story."

It seems that at the present time the public interest in the Glastonbury Zodiac and its relation to the Arthurian legends of Avalon is confined largely to individuals in Great Britain and Canada.

But there is a growing interest among persons in other parts of the world. The full implications of the epic are only gradually being realized. Soon, however, so the enthusiasts insist, the whole world will "sit up and take notice." This, at any rate, is the prediction of two of my more recent correspondents, Mrs. Evelyn Swanepoel in England and Mr. G. N. Russell of Ireland, both of whom have provided me with data that appears in the later parts of the present study. I am also deeply indebted to Winifred Babcock, President of Harold Institute, for substantial help.

In conclusion let me emphasize that the present volume can only serve as an "interim" report on the Glastonbury saga. If the Zodiac is real, and its objective existence properly verified by archaeologists, this will constitute a momentous "breakthrough," having more impact than the discovery of the Dead Sea Scrolls and the computerized confirmation of Stonehenge as an astronomical observatory. I make no predictions at this time. But it is my hope that this book will help to satisfy the growing curiosity about Somerset—this "Holyest Erthe" of Glastonbury, Camelot, and King Arthur's Avalon.

OLIVER LESLIE REISER

Pittsburgh, Pennsylvania

Invocation

THE GLASTONBURY HYMN

And did those feet in ancient time
    Walk upon England's mountains green?
And was the Holy Lamb of God
    On England's pleasant pastures seen?
And did the Countenance Divine
    Shine forth upon our clouded Hills?
And was Jerusalem builded here
    Among those dark Satanic Mills?

                  —*William Blake*

From our old books I know
That Joseph came of old to Glastonbury
And there the heathen prince, Arviragus,
Gave him an isle of marsh wherein to build:
And there he built with wattles from the marsh
A little lonely church in days of yore.

              —*Alfred Lord Tennyson*

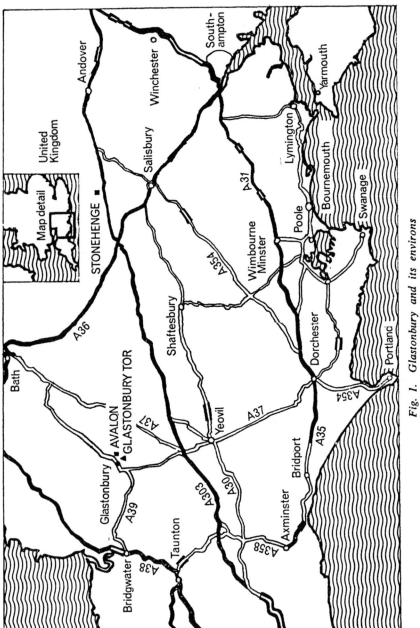

Fig. 1. Glastonbury and its environs

PART I

The Zodiac of Somerset

"We have often been told that astronomy is found in a
developed form among the ancient Babylonians, traceable
back to 3,000 B.C., but not until I discovered this 'Temple
of the Stars' in Somerset in 1925 A.D. and photographed
it from the air, have we been able to define exactly the
original features forming the Zodiac."

K. E. MALTWOOD, *The Enchantments of Britain*

(Canada, 1944, page 28)

I. THIS ENGLAND: A MAGNETIZED SPOT?

We are here about to explore what has been termed the "most
sacred spot in England." The Glastonbury Abbey, the Tor of
Avalon, the Zodiac of Somerset, the Camelot of Arthurian
romance—these constitute an epic of such awesome scope and
qualities as to render it difficult to encompass within the limits of
ordinary language. But the story must be told, and retold, until
history gets it right. And because we must strive to be thorough in
an area which ranges widely from astronomy and geography to
archæology and mythology, it is all the more essential that we
provide ourselves with the relevant background material for the
understanding of this strange and perhaps still unfinished saga.
Therefore the reader's patience is solicited as we summarize as con-
cisely as possible the history of the people and the country we shall
be dealing with in this unfolding adventure. The map opposite
gives the locale of this Odyssey.

The history of England in its earliest period is still to be written.
Some historians have portrayed the most ancient condition of the
country as one of Cimmerian darkness, the natives being pictured as
savages who lived in caves and relied on hunting and fishing for

1

food. According to this view, there were members of genus *Homo* walking the hills of Britain half a million years ago. Even though this be so, it seems that the later culture of the Cromagnons (Aurignacians) was carried over the land bridge that joined the British Isles and the Continent of Europe. The last ice-age began to disappear about 18,000 years ago, following which the North Sea swamped the bridge so that ancient Britain was geographically isolated from the Continent.

About the year 10,000 B.C., the Magdalenian culture of the Continent was transported by boat across the channel. Time and again, apparently, the people of Britain, from the earlier Stone Age to the later Christian era, were destined to be overrun by outside invaders.

In rehearsing the story of the successive waves of colonization of England, mention is inevitably made of these "outsiders." Among such were the Formorians, by way of what later was called Spain, the Nemeans and Melasians from Greece. Still later, the Beaker people and the semi-nomadic cattle-breeding Windmill Hill people infiltrated the country. Next came the Phoenicians, in their day the greatest traders in the world. They travelled across the seas in their long-oared galleys to secure tin from the Britons.

It seems obvious from this that the British, when they became known in history as a people, were a mixed race. This must be so, for the Celts, Anglo-Saxons, Normans, and others, who were warring with each other much of the time, were "mixed" even before they arrived on English soil. For example, the Saxons of Germany before their migrations to Britain, were not a "pure" race any more than their forerunners, the Proto-Nordics. Quite probably, by the time Caesar's Legions arrived in England the Britons were as "cultured" as the arrogant Roman invaders.

In addition to the difficult problems of racial and ethnic origins, there is the equally difficult problem of dating. The evidence seems to indicate that the Neolithic period began in Northwestern Europe about 3,500 B.C. However, as Gordon Childe has pointed out, there are no precise dates in the prehistory of this area and one must exercise caution in all surmises. Nevertheless, we must make some conjectures.

Celts and Iberians

Perhaps one of the biggest upheavals of peoples and cultures—"one that left nothing the same"—was the invasion of the Celts, who fanned out over the Continent of Europe and the British Isles from their point of origin. From the viewpoint of cultural impact, the Celts (or Kelts) were the first Europeans of importance north of the Alps. The Romans called them Gauls.

Today the term "Celts" in a more precise denotation tends to be restricted to the Scottish Highlanders, the Celtic (or Gaelic) Irish, the Cornish, and the inhabitants of Brittany in northern France (the Bretons). The changes in place-names has some importance. For example, what is now called Scotland acquired that name later; earlier it was called Caledonia. The classic biography, *The Life of Saint Columba*, by Saint Adamnan (A.D. 679-704), has been "Newly Translated from the Latin with Notes and Illustrations" (subtitle), by Wentworth Huyshe (First ed., London, 1905). In his notes to this volume. Mr. Huyshe points out (p. 240) that Adamnan refers to the northwestern part of what we now call Ireland as Scotia, nowhere applying that term to what we now term Scotland. This transposition to Northern Britain did not occur until 930 A.D. The Latin *Scotia* was used only as the name of Ireland, also called Hibernia.

The early Celtic inhabitants of England were acquainted with the use of bronze and, later, worked with iron. They knew how to till the soil and became an agricultural people. The language of the Celts of Wales was known as Kymric.

Customarily the cradle-land of the Celts is placed in France and Southern Germany. More recently archæologists have found evidence of the "Upper Danubian Urn Burials" dating to the thirteenth century before Christ. The latest discoveries indicate that this cradle-land must be extended east of the Alps to the region of Czechoslovakia, Northern Italy, and the Iberian peninsula (Spain); subsequently parts adjacent thereto, including the Brythons or Briton, became "Celticized." The fact that the Celts objected to writing as a substitute for word-of-mouth communication may explain the lack of script among the earliest Hibernians and Druids.

Obviously we are working in a fogbound terrain, and are not at all certain of the proper conclusions to be drawn from history,

3

archæology and anthropology. It seems established that "Iberians" was the name applied to the ancient inhabitants of Spain, who evidently preceded the Celts. The Welsh and the Basques (of Portugal) are believed to contain elements of Iberian derivations. But this still leaves us with the interesting question of the relation of the Celts and Iberians to the inhabitants of ancient Ireland, the country known to the Romans as Hibernia, but later referred to affectionately by Irish poets as *Erin*.

Some things, however, we can regard as reasonably well established. We know, for example, that there are close ties between the Celts of Brittany and the Celts of Wales and Ireland. The language still employed by the Bretons (of Brittany) is similar to such other Celtic languages as Welsh and Irish. The common lack of a written language in the early days tends to reinforce the idea, previously mentioned, of a "secret society"—the "mysteries" —among the earliest Iberians, Hibernians, and Druids.

Another interesting link between the above-mentioned peoples is the fact that Brittany contains many stone monuments and menhirs, such as are also found in England and Scotland. There are various types of stone monuments. Dolmen are stone tables of the megalithic civilization. These are sometimes shaped like pyramids. Closed dolmen were used as burial chambers. Perhaps some menhirs were phallic and fertility symbols.

The considerably more difficult problems of relating the Celtic peoples in their several branches to the half-mythical Indo-Europeans ("Aryans") is a more remote but none-the-less intriguing question. The supposition that there is a connection between the Celts of Europe and the inhabitants of Eastern Europe and Asia Minor is by no means absurd. But that "the Celtæ had among them from the remote antiquity an Order of Literati called Druids . . . "—this is somewhat more "far-fetched." And how can they be "literati," if they don't write? Nevertheless, this is exactly what Isabel Hill Elder claims in her engaging book, *Celt, Druid, and Culdee* (London, 1962, p. 87). This is part of her more general thesis that the original church of Britain was founded by the *Culdees*, "certain strangers," i.e., "Judaean refugees" who found refuge in Britain. It should be noted that in seeking to assimilate the Culdees and the Druids as integral components of English civilization Mrs. Elder is not alone. According to some sources, the earlier

4

name for Britain was "clas Merddyn," the school of Merdin, and this was associated with Druidism.

A thesis of a somewhat similar nature is propounded by Mrs. Maltwood, who urges that the aborigines of South Wales, of Cornwall, and of the Severn Valley, where the Zodiacal circle lies, were the early "Kelts," calling themselves "Khaldis" or "Chaldees" (Mrs. Elder's "Culdees"?), and related to the Iberian type. The Druids belonged to this same type, according to Mrs. Maltwood, and there must have been thousands of them in Britain —even up to Iona—to help the architect-astrologers construct the enormous earthworks of the giant effigies. Thus, whether we adopt Mrs. Elder's or Mrs. Maltwood's derivation, we find that we are in the middle of a mystery play, with the end not yet in sight.

Also we have here some broad hints of the potentially explosive nature of the subject matter we are handling. Our survey will have to be a capsulated summary of the history of Britain and that segment of the culture which we are seeking to understand. If the reader feels that some of this is irrelevant, I can assure him that this is not so. The complete story is essential to an understanding of a series of events which perhaps is without parallel in the development of human civilization. But this remains to be seen.

II. THE PLOT: A CHOSEN PEOPLE

The two quotations at the front of this book—from William Blake and Alfred Lord Tennyson—mark out several "magnetic moments" in the history of Britain which seem to reflect some unusual configurations of forces. These configurations are wholistic or gestalt phenomena of well-nigh miraculous proportions—or so at any rate others have believed.

To produce a "magnetic moment in human history" requires a *place*, a *people* with a *culture*, and a *time* on the earth. In this instance, the *place* is Avalon's Tor Hill and its physical environs—the Camelot of Arthur's Somerset. The *people* in sequential order are of the several main historical eras—from the ancient Celts and Druids to the later Britons who passed over the bridge provided by Arthur's "Round Table" to the Glastonbury Abbey and the medieval monks who lived there. The story is brought up-to-date in the twentieth century uncovering of the Avalonian Zodiac as discovered by Katherine Maltwood. This immense saga covers a long period of time—almost 5,000 years, it is claimed. It seems well-nigh incredible that one spot on the earth should be the lens-like focus of such a configuration of forces and events. Perhaps it is for the foregoing reasons that Glastonbury became known as the "most sacred spot in England."

In attempting to weave the strands of mythology, history, and prophecy into a unitary pattern, one finds it natural to echo the refrain of the stage-play of *Camelot*—"a once and future king"—except that one is then inclined to paraphrase the passage into—"a once and future Holy Land!" This indicates something of the mixed moods that are apt to characterize the students who approach this weird and eerie domain. The material is complex, obscure in many spots, and always baffling.

Also, as one goes in search of a theory, one becomes aware of a growing danger—the tendency on the part of the student to yield to the "chosen people" way of thinking. This is evident in those enthusiasts who revel in the prophecy that someday, in this land of enchantments, the Founder of Christianity will come again—in person—as allegedly he did in his earlier years as a boy. Indeed, when the question arises—as in time it will—*Why England?*, some doubtless will yield to the inclination to reply in terms of the doctrines of the "British Israelites." It is as if these historiographers are insisting that Jesus will return to fulfill some mission, so that England, now fallen as a world empire, will arise and reclaim her spiritual destiny, whatever that may be.

We have mentioned the urge to succumb to the "chosen people" delusion. This is the social analogue of the "messiah complex." But in truth, when you face up to it, the messianic mission theme may perhaps be given some plausibility, provided it is interpreted to mean that in various times and places on the surface of the earth there have been a number of "chosen people"—chosen not by some anthropomorphic god but by the "world sensorium" or by Teilhard de Chardin's *Noosphere*, if that is your preference. So what we then have is a "chosen people" at a "chosen place" at some "chosen time," as this is illustrated in my article on this topic.[1] This configuration of time-place-people-teacher moves over the surface of the globe like an electric sign over a bank of lights. This means, of course, that a linear or elementalistic theory of history is faulty and must give way to a wholistic or non-linear approach to history. Whatever one's own predilections, the scholar is under obligation to uncover and report the story as objectively as possible, and I therefore restrain my own preferences as best I can. However, some tentative commitments must be made as foundation stones, if any edifice is to emerge toward the end of our constructions. The very fact that the climate of opinion is changing in England is significant, and before launching into an exposition of the Maltwood claims, let us say a word about this change in attitude.

Among the scholars in England who have studied this psychological metamorphosis, there are several who have informed me that while the original attitude was that the Zodiac story was a ridiculous fairy-tale, the climate of opinion is changing rapidly. In the decades of the nineteen thirties and forties Mrs. Maltwood's ideas were poorly received, for a variety of reasons. She could not find anyone of recognized standing to investigate her claims. It was too much for the conservative English. There had always been bitter fights over the alleged coming of the early Christian leaders to Glastonbury. And this "Zodiac thing" was even worse. People said that Mrs. Maltwood made it up, and that, in any case, no Middle Eastern people ever got so far West at the date she proposed. Of course, as we know now, evidence on this latter point has changed in recent decades, as one discovers by investigation of the ancient tombs of New Grange and others on the Boyne river in Eire. This latter material is beautifully assembled in the volume, *New Grange* (1964), by S. P. ÓRiordáin and Glyn Daniel, and I shall have occasion to refer to this work at a later point.

III. THE DISCOVERY OF THE ZODIAC

Those who know their Blavatsky (Madame Blavatsky is frequently referred to as H. P. B.) claim that she asserted that initiates from Egypt went out as missionaries to the four quarters of the world and made four zodiacs. If this is so, there are still three to be discovered.

The discovery of the Glastonbury Zodiac in Somerset, England, was made by Katherine Maltwood in 1925. According to one who

7

knew Mrs. Maltwood, the discovery came to her as "one of those flashes of insight that come to genius." In Mrs. Maltwood's own words, "I shall never forget my utter amazement when the truth dawned on me that the outline of a lion was drawn by the curves of the Cary river, below the old capital town of Somerset." This she tells us in her book, *The Enchantments of Britain* (1944, p. 81).

Mrs. Maltwood at the time of this discovery was retracing the quests of King Arthur's Knights for the Holy Grail. She formed the impression that the Knights followed each other in a circle through similar adventures with the same mighty beasts. The "effigies"—as Mrs. Maltwood terms them—correspond to the twelve figures of the Zodiac, the center of this vast Zodiac being Butleigh (meaning the "center of the wheel"!). Her eventual theory was that the area around Glastonbury—a circle of ten miles in diameter and thirty miles in circumference—depicted the effigies or "signs" of the heavenly zodiac of the Milky Way galaxy. It was claimed that ten of these could be identified without difficulty and the two others were not so clearly discernible. A marked feature of the whole design is that the heads of eleven figures are turned toward the West, the sunset (for the equinoctial line between Aldebaran and Antares, two stars in the celestial zodiac, runs West and East).

The figures on the face of the earth are outlined by ancient tracks, by waterways, by contours of earthworks upon the ground—some of these natural and some artificial or man-made. On the basis of these considerations, Mrs. Maltwood arrived at her hypothesis about the "Temple of the Stars" mapped out on the surface of the earth.

Further research only served to fortify and confirm in Mrs. Maltwood's mind this seemingly fantastic hypothesis. *If a planisphere is placed behind an ordnance survey map and the stars and constellations are pricked through, they are found to fall on or near their counterparts* on the ground. Pilots have reported on them from the air, and some good aerial photographs have been taken. Thus it does appear that some very early people of Britain mapped out a "heaven on earth," as it has been called.

We have reported on the early reactions to these claims. Mrs. Maltwood's ideas were ridiculed as preposterous. Today there are a number of research groups engaged in studying these complex problems. Professor Philip Rahtz of Birmingham University directs the "digs" at Tor Hill. His map of the Island of Glastonbury gives some idea of his type of research (see Fig. 2 overleaf). The enthusiasm of the general public for this type of involvement is indicated in the photograph that forms plate I. Others have assumed the task of correlating the tales of the classic *High History of the Holy Grail* with the constellations as marked out geographically in and around Glastonbury, each Arthurian episode being assigned its appropriate constellation. And there's the rub! For reasons to be given later, Mrs. Maltwood claims that the Zodiac was constructed about 2,700 B.C.—a thousand years before the earliest construction of Stonehenge. *But how could King Arthur's Knights, more than 3,000 years later, have enacted the drama of a plot mapped out on the vast vale of Avalon—when they didn't even know about the Zodiac under their very feet?*

Did the builders of the Zodiac have a pre-cognition of something to come at a later stage? Or contrariwise, did the Knights of the "Table Round" have a retro-cognition enabling them symbolically to re-enact a drama on a stage as big as Somerset's "Temple"? Or have we here merely the workings of a tremendous fantasy of self-deception, rather than an international mystery play of awesome import?

If her claims are substantiated, it surely is obvious that Mrs. Maltwood's investigations have uncovered something of immense value, quite beyond that of an isolated episode of history. The problem of the significance of these discoveries lies in the direction and meaning they provide for the guidance of human evolution, i.e., what the implications are for the past, present, and future development of mankind. In any event, it is now clear that the message of the Avalonian Zodiac is much too big for one individual to handle alone. Mrs. Maltwood asked for help—and didn't receive it. Today we realize that the problems she opened up lead to an interdisciplinary project of immense proportions, requiring for its resolution a knowledge of astronomy, astrology, archæology, anthropology, folklore, history—even esotericism. Beyond all these, there will be needed the cooperation of keepers of archives all over Europe, if not of America and Asia too. Experts in the studies of ancient languages (Irish, Welsh, Basque, Old French, Hebrew, Aramaic,

9

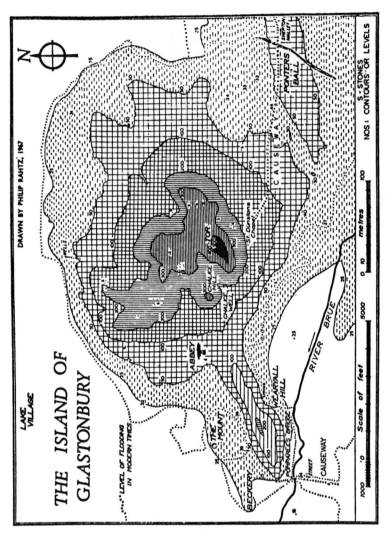

Fig. 2. The Island of Glastonbury. The map shows the position of all the places where digging has taken place, or will in the future. It also shows their relationship to the heights of each above sea level, and the extent to which Glastonbury would have been a true island, depending on the sea level at various times. It will be seen that a sea level of about 32 feet above the present one would cut off Glastonbury completely, except for the narrow neck of land on the east side which is spanned by the great earthwork of Ponters Ball. (Map by courtesy of P.A. Rahtz, Birmingham University.)

Akkadian, Greek, etc.) will have their contributions to make. The mystery will be revealed, if it ever is, in the coming era of mankind. But what *is* the mystery of Glastonbury? And where and how does it fit into the scheme of other mysteries: Greek, Egyptian, Scandinavian, Tibetan, and the rest? According to Elizabeth Leader, one of the prominent students in this field, the Zodiac is a great international heritage. To rediscover and explain, and set in proper context, the vast learning behind the great design—this, she says, will be a monumental undertaking. The problem of confirming the Somerset Zodiac by scientific methodologies will require *old* ordnance maps to recover earlier markings, and good air-views of the entire area. Many of the ancient roads may still be there, but built over during later centuries. New shrubbery and trees, and receding water ways have modified the original landscape and seascape of the Cornish part of England. (See Fig. 2). But the allurements are there and the rewards of success are fabulous.

When all the contemporary groups, sometimes referred to as the "New Company of Avalon," are working in harmony, it may be possible to test the truth of the legends, the history, and the prophecies. Today there is great interest in the giant Zodiac as the sacred centre of a breath-taking drama, linking the themes of the Holy Grail and the Temple of the Stars, the Cauldron of Unfailing Supply. After all—so it is said—the Grail is what we are all seeking. Here one thinks once more of Tennyson's lines in *The Holy Grail*:

"... now the Holy Thing is here again
Among us, brother
That so perchance the vision may be seen
By thee and those, and all the world be heal'd."

To see whether indeed we can find the "Grail," we must next become better acquainted with Mrs. Katherine E. Maltwood and the places wherein all this occurred.

IV. THE MALTWOOD SAGA

Katherine E. Maltwood was born in England in 1878 and died in Canada in 1961. From her portrait which is reproduced in Pl. II, one can see that she was a most beautiful and impressive lady.

11

While in England, she and her husband, John Maltwood, lived in Somerset. Their home was at Chilton Priori on the Polden Hills, about eight miles from Glastonbury. It was in the turret of this home that Mrs. Maltwood did much of her writing. Here, too, the husband and wife could look out over the lovely countryside in this storied spot of England. Behind the Priori is the old village of Childen Polden.

The Maltwoods left Somerset in 1935, and after extensive travels turned to Canada, where they settled in 1938. On Vancouver Island in British Columbia they purchased a replica of a 14th century Tudor hall, furnished it with early English furniture, and converted it into a library and a home for the arts. It is now the Maltwood Museum and the property of the University of Victoria in British Columbia. Two views are shown in Pl. III. At this Museum— formerly affectionately known as "the Thatch"—one may view Mrs. Maltwood's own works of art, as well as the Chinese, Asian, Persian, and other works of art. Mrs. Maltwood was a distinguished artist in her own right. In her earlier years many of her creations had been exhibited in London art galleries. In addition to this however, she was a great collector, and the Maltwood art treasures are now on exhibit at the Museum, open to the public. The novel, *The House of Fulfillment*, by L. Adams Beck, is in part the story of Mrs. Maltwood's life.

V. THE PLACE—GLASTONBURY AND AVALON

Britain is rich in early monuments and romantic legends, many of which tie her in with antiquity. But of all the visible links with the ancient past, the town of Glastonbury offers the most enthralling evidences of ties with generations of men long since departed. It is at the very center of Arthur's West Country. (See Fig. 3).

The town of Glastonbury lies in the heart of Somerset. This area is redolent with legends and history. Stonehenge, not far distant, is only 90 miles from London, while Glastonbury itself is approximately 143 miles from that city. This general area contains Cornwall and the Cornish coast, beauty spots of England that are celebrated in mythology, tradition, and history. In the early times

12

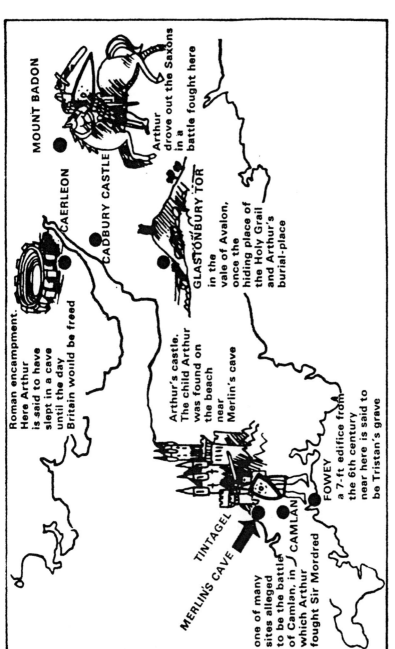

MOUNT BADON

Arthur drove out the Saxons in a battle fought here

CAERLEON

CADBURY CASTLE

GLASTONBURY TOR

in the vale of Avalon, once the hiding place of the Holy Grail and Arthur's burial-place

Roman encampment. Here Arthur is said to have slept in a cave until the day Britain would be freed

Arthur's castle. The child Arthur was found on the beach near Merlin's cave

FOWEY

a 7-ft edifice from the 6th century near here is said to be Tristan's grave

TINTAGEL

MERLIN'S CAVE

CAMLAN

one of many sites alleged to be the battle of Camlan, in which Arthur fought Sir Mordred

Fig. 3. Arthur's West Country

Cornwall was noted for its copper mines and tin, these having been worked from times unremembered.

In the earliest period some of the territory surrounding Glastonbury lay beneath the sea. There are even stories of ships unloading cargoes at Glastonbury. In time geological forces elevated the land; later this area became a Druid center; and still later it formed the center of a sacred Christian shrine—a kind of second Jerusalem—only to be desecrated when, toward the end, the Tor Hill was converted into a gibbet for the hanging of an Abbot by a murderous king.

We have mentioned that the Celts and the Druids were among the early inhabitants of Somerset. How long they resided there before their ways were disturbed by outsiders—among whom one always thinks of the Romans—is not known. Of course, the problem of the origin of the Celts is still before us.

But certainly these early Celtic Druids must have had a part in the utilization, if not the construction, of the Tor. Which is illustrated in Plate IV. It has been suggested that the terraced paths on the slopes of the Glastonbury Hill, upon which the Tower is situated, were the processional paths of the Druids, the ways whereby the Druids climbed the Hill presumably to worship the sun and perhaps also—as they believed—to rise above the evil spirits below.

It also appears that the village of Somerset used this area as a cemetery, some of the dead bodies being buried atop the Tor Hill; in any case, and in harmony with the Druidic doctrine of immortality (apparently similar to the Hindu-Pythagorean doctrine of metempsychosis), it was supposed that the spirits of the departed had to pass through the Tor. How well this fits with Mrs. Maltwood's theses is an open question.

Glastonbury itself is situated on rising ground, and this was known as the Isle of Avalon. Some have supposed that Glastonbury was a peninsula with perhaps a harbour for ships. The word "Avalon" is of uncertain origin, but perhaps derived from the Welsh word for apple, thus indicative of an orchard island ("where the cider comes from"). Other derivations have also been offered.

The origin of the name "Glastonbury" is also guess work. *YNNIS WITRIN*, an ancient Celtic name for Glastonbury, means the "Crystal Island," while Glastonbury referred to the "Fortress of Glass." Another theory is that the name is derived from *Glaesting-*

Plate I. Archaeological research on Tor Hill.

Plate II. Katherine E. Maltwood.

(a)

(b)

Plate III. Two views of the Maltwood Museum (a) Side view (b) Front view. The Museum was built in the style of a 14th Century Hall House and opened on the occasion of the visit to Victoria of Their Gracious Majesties King George VI and Queen Elizabeth, May 30th 1939.

Plate IV. Tor Hill

aburgh, the hill fortress of Glaestings. In any case according to Mrs. Maltwood, the Isle of Avalon was known throughout Europe as the "Island of the Blest" and the place of the departed spirits. All this allows us to surmise that Glastonbury was perhaps (or assuredly) the abode of the dead, encircled by a wall of glass.

We see here, once more, how history and mythology are bathed in mysticism. Nevertheless, there is a persistent, though muddy or jumbled, belief concerning Avalon (or Avallu) as a Western Eden. There are references in Chaldean *Gilgamesh* literature to Avallu, the wonderful apple-garden of the West, with its tree of life. Celtic poetry abounds in references to the mystical character of its apple trees. These stories are paralleled in Greek myths about the Garden of the Hesperides from which Hercules won the apple of wisdom. Whether, more precisely, the "starry firmament" of the *Creation Epic* of Babylonian folklore is in any way a reference to the Zodiac is a matter for speculation.

However long the original inhabitants of Somerset may have enjoyed their isolation, it was not destined to last forever. Various invaders, including the Roman legions, were hammering on their doors. The introduction of Christianity was connected with the coming of St. Joseph of Arimathea and his disciples, so legend tells us. According to the story, after burying the body of Christ, Joseph brought the Holy Grail and the Chalice of the Last Supper to England, where he then founded the first Christian church. Here, legend has it, the pagan king, Arviragus, presented the famous Hides of Land of Glastonbury to St. Joseph, a most remarkable act of hospitality. It has been suggested that these amicable relations reflected an earlier contact when St. Joseph previously had visited England in his role as a tin merchant. If so, it is not at all surprising that the "Oaks of Avalon"—named "Gog" and "Magog"—should have been planted in memory of the landing of St. Joseph and his eleven companions.

Joseph, Jesus, and Glastonbury

The several legends and traditions about early Christianity in England are so intriguing that, at the risk of repetition, it is well to elaborate a bit.

As we have mentioned, legend states that Jesus visited the country of Somerset with his uncle (or great uncle), Joseph of Arimathea,

15

during the childhood years of Jesus. To Glastonbury, legend also tells us, Joseph returned with his small band of refugees, to escape persecution in Palestine after the crucifixion. It may be that Somerset as a "magnetic spot" drew the exiled followers of the Messiah to the only place where they would be accepted by those who still knew the ancient wisdom. Of course, it is also possible that, after the fall of Jerusalem and the exodus of the Jews (the *Diaspora*), there may have been some remnants of the Essene brotherhood. In this connection one recalls the story of the two sea-borne Marys to Provence —the two sisters, Mary of Nazareth and Mary Magdalene.

This certainly is treading on thin ice. Equally frail and unsubstantiated is the tradition that St. Mary, mother of Jesus, came to Britain with St. Joseph of Arimathea, her uncle. This, were it true, would mean that the Blessed Virgin was the thirteenth of the group headed by St. Joseph. Even more astounding is the claim made by some that the Blessed Virgin lies buried somewhere in Avalon ("Isle

GLASTONBURY ABBEY RECONSTRUCTED

Fig. 4

of the Departed Spirits"!), perhaps more precisely in St. Mary's of the old Wattle Church. Those interested in this problem may consult the book, *St. Joseph of Arimathea at Glastonbury*, by the Rev. Lionel S. Lewis (1964, Appendix 8).

Concerning the founding of the Wattle Church, so frequently mentioned in the literature, opinions differ; but apparently it was considered so "sacred" that many Saxon churches were built around it. Of course, the Glastonbury Abbey itself is its institutional re-

16

incarnation, as it were. (See Fig. 4). It is interesting to note that in Mrs. Maltwood's view the Wattle Church—later the Glastonbury Abbey—was built upon the tail of the Phoenix (of the Zodiac). The link between the ancient wisdom of the Zodiac and the newer teachings of the Christ was forged at this very spot where the Glastonbury chapel and the Tor stand together in Avalon—the sign of Aquarius, the blending of the old and the new, as Mrs. Maltwood saw it. If this is correct, this "Holyest Erthe" of Somerset was hallowed ground long before the early Christians settled there.

Strangely enough, in Bligh Bond's book, *The Gate of Remembrance*, there is a reference (p.147) to a zodiac on the floor of "ye Mary Chappel . . . that all might see and understand the mystery." But just what this "mystery" may be is itself a mystery. At any rate, there still lingers on the idea of some antecedent wisdom religion which influenced the Druids, the Pythagoreans, the Essenes, and St. Joseph and his followers. This field of wide-open speculation goes far beyond any presently available facts at our disposal.

One should not be surprised that the monks, who were domiciled here, were ignorant of all this "pre-history" as we have attempted to uncover it—or else they were indifferent to it. They built the Chapel of St. Michael on the top of Tor Hill, where the remains of their own Druidic predecessors were interred. One may anticipate that, sooner or later, the imaginative students in this field will try to make something of the fact—or supposition—that the hill of the Tor is reminiscent of Mount Tabor, this latter still called the Hill of Tor by the Arabs who inhabit that land.

Chalice Hill and Well

It is difficult to tear one's self away from the Tor—it dominates the mind as it dominates the landscape. In a moment I shall return to the Tor. Meantime, let us turn for a moment to the two "satellites of the Tor," namely, Chalice Hill and Weary-all Hill. The latter promontory is supposedly the spot where St. Joseph of Arimathea and his followers rested after their long journey from the eastern Holy Land to Britain. Chalice Hill, close by, is celebrated in legend as the place where Joseph buried the Holy Cup of the Last Supper, when he and his companions took sanctuary there. Also from this spot one may proceed to the Chalice Well. Some believe that the

Holy Grail will be found here in the "Blood Spring." This two-chambered well may originally have been a Druidic well (of Egyptian design, some say); in any case, it pours forth its never-ending healing waters—at the foot of the Tor of St. Michael!

We have already mentioned the theory of the origin of the name of Weary-all Hill. From the summit of the Hill, with its grand panorama of the Vale of Avalon, one can look out over the broad plains stretching to the Mendips and the Distant Quantocks. The picturesque Avalonian hills are naturally tied in with early sacred history. This is said to be the spot where St. Joseph placed his hawthorn staff in the ground, which immediately took root and blossomed to become the famous Holy Thorn of Glastonbury, year after year putting forth its flowers on Christmas day in honour of the Nativity.

Of course, the St. Joseph tradition and all that goes with it has been belittled by the skeptical scholars who have asserted that this—like Arthur's Knights and the Holy Grail legends—was a medieval invention by the Glastonbury monks for purposes of attracting more pilgrims . . . And so the battle rages!

The Tor

We now return to the Glastonbury Tor, a structure of peculiar fascination to all members of the "New Company of Avalon." Accordingly, as Mrs. Maltwood puts it in her *Itinerary of the Somerset Giants*—"Come with me, 500 feet up Castle Hill, to gaze over the 'forbidden Land of Logres,' and drink of the mystery and enchantment of this 'Cauldron of Wisdom,' whilst the sun sinks down into the western sea only to rise again as King Arthur in the Golden Dawn."

At the summit of Tor Hill stands the Tower of St. Michael's Church, 525 feet above the sea. Only the massive tower—an empty shell restored in 1804—remains standing. The tower was at the west end of the church. It is a three-storied structure (as can be seen from Plate I) with an embattled parapet. Remaining in the tower are belfrey windows, the lancet windows, and the west doorway, above which are two panels, the one representing St. Michael weighing a soul against the devil, the other perhaps representing St. Bridget. The upper stories contain some niches, in one of which are replicas of the feet of St. George and the head of the slain dragon.

18

The interior of the tower is open to the public. One of the distinguished visitors was Major Tudor-Pole, chairman of the Chalice Well Trust, who climbed the hill and entered the tower. To his surprise, Major Tudor-Pole found inscribed inside the tower these words: *"Christ stood here."* This fits in with the ancient tradition that Jesus as a youth visited Glastonbury with his uncle, Joseph of Arimathea. Of course, this does not prove the ancient legend. There are other scribbles to be seen on the walls.

Here one must pause for an observation. One of the remarkable things in this wondrous tale of fact and fable is the manner in which St. Joseph bridges the gap that separates past and future. Observe the nexus: on the one hand, as already indicated, Joseph and his companions brought Christianity to Britain. On the other hand, St. Joseph is inextricably linked to King Arthur—a span of half a millennium—whose lineage supposedly can be traced back to St. Joseph. Every one of the Twelve Knights of the Round Table claimed descent from St. Joseph (or it has been claimed for them). I don't know whether it has ever been pointed out, but St. Joseph stands in pretty much the same relation to the twelve anchorites (they apparently were housed in the *Anchorage*) that Arthur does to the Twelve Knights.

What this may prove with respect to Mrs. Maltwood's thesis relative to the Zodiac in the Avalonian hills is not clear. Her far-ranging interpretations could be regarded as the symbolic interpretation of some ancient astrological-geographical-archæological facts. This is surely a unique configuration of forces. But there are some literary precedents for these speculations.

In his book, *Celtic Researches* (1804), Edward Davies sought to establish the links between the Zodiacal lore, the ancient British priesthood, and the Arthurian cycle. This included not only the Druid priests, but supposedly went back even to Sumer-Chaldean priests and astrologers whose zodiacal myths had the sun-god escaping death in a sacred ship. Then, somehow, in history the Round Zodiac became the Round Table. Thus the alchemy of myth-making is perpetually at work.

The Place

Much of the "continuity" in Mrs. Maltwood's thinking remains to be articulated. Among the literary remains preserved at the Malt-

19

wood Museum are hundreds of letters and notes (see the list at the end of this volume). One of the items uncovered by Mrs. Mary E. Allan is a small aerial photograph of the Tor, with a notation on the back reading: "Isle of Avalon—1930 Zodiacal Figure. Isle of Avalon was to take its place at the Round Table as the Water-Carrier." The second item noted was this: "Somerset Zodiac was the *first* of the mighty labours of Britain—Stonehenge was the *second*." If one were inclined to be fanciful, it might be predicted that this land of Britain contains within itself the nascent form of a New Jerusalem, so that the prophecy of William Blake will assuredly be fulfilled. This, presumably, as Mrs. Maltwood might have put it, will be the *third* of the mighty labours of Britain.

Also among Mrs. Maltwood's notes at the Museum is a memo concerning the Zodiacal Phoenix, which she had superimposed on the map of the Glastonbury Tor, and this led her to the conclusion that "the effigy of the evangelistic Eagle or Phoenix is seen here drinking from the famous Druid Well. The Tor forming the bird's head is 500 feet high . . . The Eagle thus forms the celebrated *Island of Avalon* (on Tor Hill)." (see Fig. 5).

It needs to be kept in mind that the Phoenix was the precursor of Aquarius. The sign of Aquarius or Water Carrier in this giant Zodiac is spread over the top and sides of Tor Hill, to correspond to the constellations of Aquarius in the heavens. In ancient days, apparently, the sign of Aquarius, the Water Carrier with the tipped vessel, was known also as the *Phoenix*. (See Fig. 6). But now we see that it has also come to be called the "eagle". By any name, it signifies the outpouring of the spirit upon the earth.

All this—looked at from any angle—is a remarkable congeries of phenomena. The architects of the Zodiac, whoever they were, constructed this immense calendar of the sun through its apparent path around the galactic constellations of the Milky Way, about 2,700 B.C., according to Mrs. Maltwood, using the land of the sea moors of Somerset for the elevated Zodiacal figures. Probably any causeways connecting them (the original ones) have long since disappeared (however, see Mrs. Caine's views as given later). But enough is left of the original pattern to show the mosaic of the Temple of the Stars—the "Cauldron of Wisdom," the "Caer Sidi of the Cymry," or the "Round Table of the Logres" in Arthurian legend. Until Katherine Maltwood lifted the "mantle of invisibility," the mosaic

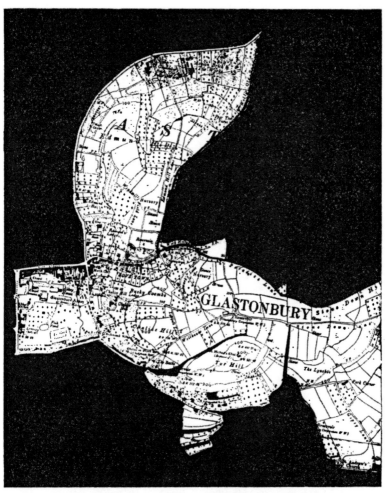

Fig. 5. The Isle of Avalon as Aquarius. The Effigy Phoenix flying towards the Sunrise turns its head to drink from the Blood Spring, which is the CUP OF THIS AQUARIUS.

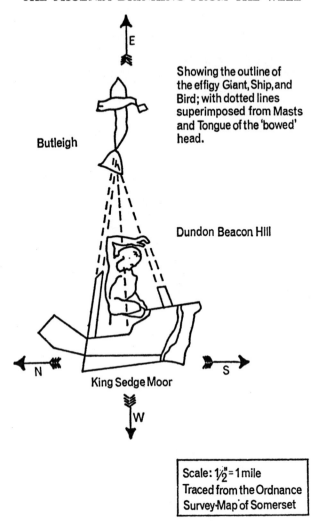

Showing the outline of
the effigy Giant, Ship, and
Bird; with dotted lines
superimposed from Masts
and Tongue of the 'bowed'
head.

Butleigh

Dundon Beacon Hill

King Sedge Moor

Scale: 1/2" = 1 mile
Traced from the Ordnance
Survey Map of Somerset

Fig. 6. The 'Phoenix' — drinking from the well

It is a curious fact that the Phoenix is also identified with the Eagle. In the Maltwood "Bible Box" there is a photograph which states, on the back, that "the effigy of the Evangelistic Eagle as Phoenix is seen here drinking from the famous Druid Well. The Tor forming the bird's head is 500 feet high, and being nearer the camera looks larger in proportion to the wings and tail which slopes downward to almost sea level." At a later stage in this discussion, there will be more to report on Orion —the Giant effigy, whose "ear" takes on a peculiar importance in Katherine Maltwood's theory.

had lain hidden. Whoever the builders may have been, the sun worshippers of 5,000 years ago must have been numerous and skillful. These effigies are of considerable size. According to Mrs. Maltwood, eight of them are approximately of the same measurements—6,000 yards—and this supposedly confirms that they could not have been fortuitous. Some figures certainly are archaic, i.e., natural formations, and some obviously artificial or man-made. With respect to the natural outlines, such as the Cary river contour, it is almost as if the earth itself assisted in the formation of these effigies!

What is lacking to confirm the deliberate design of the "signs" are the "markers" for the design. But it is quite possible that in the process of draining the whole district, they may have been obliterated, or in time they may have sunk into the ground—This in spite of the fact that the designers of the mosaic demonstrated a superior knowledge of irrigation and earthwork construction. This latter, to some students, suggests the influence of the civilization of the ancient Euphrates river valley.

So much for the immediate focus of our survey. As one enlarges his purview of the area, it becomes evident that within a radius of 25 miles of Glastonbury are many places of great interest, not only to tourists but serious students as well. On the outskirts of town, there is an old tithe barn, known as the Abbot's barn, built about the year 1420, and still in good condition. It is a great cruciform building and resembles more a church than a monastic granary.

Two miles southwest of Glastonbury stands Sharpham Manor, built by Abbot Beere in the early days. A peculiar interest attaches to this manor inasmuch as it was the place where the aged Abbot Whiting—the last of the abbots of Glastonbury—was arrested. His trial was held at Wells in 1539, this then being followed by his execution on the summit of the Tor.

As is generally known, Cadbury Hill is not far distant from Glastonbury—a dozen miles approximately. This is accepted as the site of King Arthur's castle. The river Camel runs close by Camelot. No view compares with that obtained from the high hill of South Cadbury. Here from the ruins of the castle of Camelot one can see all over the country, as far out as the Bristol channel.

If one tries to ascend the hill of Cadbury castle by way of the footpath, this turns out to be arduous. The ruins of the old castle are still there. The walls around it are 40 feet high. Some visitors, perhaps with unusual sensitivity, feel that there must be a potent spiritual force resident in this place, for at blessed moments at eventide one can in the quiet feel a great peace, as if—so it is said—there were some serene spirit present to soothe the anxious heart. Also, it is claimed, there are strange lights that come and go at all seasons of the year. With these ghostly gleamings we leave Camelot for the moment.

It should be noted, however, that excavations are still proceeding, at Camelot as well as at Glastonbury's Tor. In connection with the Tor diggings, remains have been found of a Norman church, a Saxon church, and pre-Christian ruins. A tiny effigy of a bronze head was also found, this presumably is indicative of a Sumerian influence in the area. Beyond that, skeletons have been found of bodies buried north-to-south, tending to confirm the belief in the earlier presence of a Celtic civilization. Thus Father Time over-lays the remains of fallen and decayed peoples and cultures, long since departed.

VI.   DATING THE SOMERSET ZODIAC

The Glastonbury Zodiac is like a vast organism, with tentacles stretching out in many directions. In the dimension of time, there is the baffling problem of how and when to date the giant mosaic. The suggestion that the magician Merlin was the designer is of course not in the least helpful—unless one holds that Merlin and Arthur were archetypal figures who lived far back in pre-Christian times.

According to Mrs. Maltwood, the builders of the Glastonbury Zodiac had nothing to do with the erection of the neighboring constructions at Stonehenge and Avebury, since the Glastonbury Zodiac was erected 1,000 years earlier. Obviously, if Mrs. Maltwood's dating is ever verified, this will have important implications for history and archæology.

Mrs. Maltwood assigned the date of 2,700 B.C. for the construction of the Zodiac, this because the sun was then in Taurus, in terms of the arrangement of the "signs." One of the interesting things about the Taurus effigy is the importance of the eye of the Bull (Taurus), for it is through this eye that the equinoctial line passes about the year 2,700 B.C. (as brought out in Plate V).

As previously noted, another effigy of special interest is Aquarius. As Katherine Maltwood informs us:

"The Water-Bearer effigy of Glastonbury's Isle of Avalon, resembles a Phoenix with outstretched wings, turning its head to reach the life-giving water of Chalice Well Blood Spring; for the Druids' well forms the Urn of this Aquarius, and has always been associated with the Holy Grail. That being so, the astronomical point of view throws considerable light on it, for the Aquarius Cup receives the rays of the sun at the Winter Solstice, and those of the moon at the Summer Solstice, about 3,000 B.C."

For a picture of the Aquarius effigy, see Mrs. Maltwood's sketch in *A Guide to Glastonbury's Temple of the Stars*. (See Fig. 5).

The rationale of the identification of the Phoenix (or Eagle) with the sign of Aquarius is a bit obscure. But if it proves nothing else, the presence of a bird in the Zodiacal constellations seems to indicate a non-Christian origin of the design, for there are no birds present in the ancient Christian and Roman pictures of the Zodiac. According to Mrs. Maltwood, this figure is at least as old as Sargon II, King of Assyria, and the Medean god Ahura Mazda.

It may be that Katherine Maltwood allows her imagination free rein when she informs us that the "Eagle" or "Phoenix," set high on the Tor, was the symbol of the sun. Here, too, on Glastonbury Tor, "King Arthur's spirit still broods, on the wings of the Phoenix that hover over the 'elixir of life' springing from the Blood Well." In her book, *The Enchantments of Britain* (1944, pages 44-45), Mrs. Maltwood compares the Glastonbury Phoenix to the mythical bird of India, Garuda, "for it carries the cup of regeneration . . . whilst spread out below lies his 'Wheel of Time' or Chakra." This divine bird is related to the Assyrian background.

Quite clearly, from this viewpoint Aquarius *is* Glastonbury—the Abbey, Tor, Chalice Well, and all. Moreover, since astrologically the present age is turning into the Zodiacal sign of Aquarius (therefore the "Aquarian Age"), the water bearer effigy points to something imminent—the pouring out of the knowledge that mankind needs, i.e., the sharing of the physical and the spiritual resources of the world. This type of prophecy opens up vistas quite beyond our present expectations. Thus legend and history pledge a bond of fealty to the rebirth of the tradition of a celestial pattern on terrestrial contours.

25

We have seen that the Somerset Zodiac consists of 12 signs in a circle, with the heads of the effigies facing westward while the bodies remain as if revolving around a central point on the hub. From what has preceded, the student may come to the conclusion that the evidence for the hypothesis is not at this point very convincing. This is especially true if one keeps in mind that in her book, *A Guide to Glastonbury's Temple of the Stars*, Mrs. Maltwood provides a diagram of the "Pilgrim's Path Through the Effigy Signs of the Zodiac," with the interpolations of the legendary names suggested for the actors who "personify" the effigies. The point to be raised here by hostile critics is that the matching of the effigies *dramatis personæ*, with congruent event-patterns, requires a good deal of imagination—too much, the skeptics will aver.

And so additional—and independent—confirmation is much to be desired. There are several possible forms of this "convergence of evidence." One of them has to do with the "markers," already referred to, which hopefully may have survived the ravages of time. I shall return to that matter in just a moment. The other line of evidence has to do with "carbon dating" and related ways of getting at the time dimension. In this latter instance, I have some suggestions which come from Mrs. Mary Caine via a series of letters.

Mrs. Caine, while a student and disciple of Katherine Maltwood, is no sycophant. For example, she was not satisfied with Mrs. Maltwood's picturization of Scorpio and discovered a new one. She also finds a snake or serpent, close to her Scorpio. Having thus established her independence of mind as a researcher, she proceeds to search for evidence in support of the Zodiac dating. She writes me as follows:

"In favour of Mrs. Maltwood's dating we have several other factors. The three prehistoric settlements which outlie the Zodiac enclosing it in a significant equilateral triangle and lying miles apart from each other are Alfred's Burrow southwest, Glastonbury Tor, north, and Cadbury Castle, the traditional Camelot, southeast. The roads connecting each with the others form the bulk of the roads outlining the effigies—thus the age of all at one stroke. I don't remember Mrs. Maltwood making this point, but I feel it is a telling one.

"Another point which emerged after her book is equally satisfactory. Professor Coles of Cambridge, digging a little west of Glastonbury at Shapswick Heath, discovered causeway roads—a double layer of logs buried in the peat. These were carbon dated and were found to have been felled about 2,800 B.C.! . . . But it seems to me that our labour loving ancestors would hardly go to all that trouble to join two mournful and uninhabited bits of bog together . . . Obviously these roads ran from the coast to settlements in Avalon-Glastonbury among them. As far as I know, this is the only carbon dating that can be advanced to show the age of the Zodiac. Professor Waddell (*Phoenician Origin of Britons, Scots, and Welsh*) has much to say about these adventurers, claiming that Sargon's ships were already berthing in Cornish Somerset parts in 2,800 B.C."

So much, momentarily, for Mrs. Mary Caine's contributions. Now to return to the "markers."

In the earlier stages the members of the "London Group" were looking for "markers," i.e., stones that serve as "hallmarks" (as at Avebury) and these were not found. More recently Mr. John G. Bennett has informed me that an 80-year old ordnance survey of Glastonbury has been found (25 inches to the mile) and in this map a large number of menhirs or marking stones appear, many of which subsequently were removed. These menhirs form a number of alignments that have astronomical significance. It certainly seems reasonable to suppose that if there was an astronomical pattern at Glastonbury, the builders would have put in menhirs to mark certain critical points and directions. It seems now that they did exist in earlier times, and in great profusion.

The next thing to do is to get the alignments of stones plotted out and the cosines measured, so that the whole thing can be put into a computer. What the results will be cannot be predicted at this moment. So far as I can discover, Katherine Maltwood does not make much of the "markers," but doubtless she would be thrilled with this new type of confirmation, if and when it comes, and she were here to know about it.

VII.   THE PURPOSE OF THE ZODIAC

The theory that Mrs. Maltwood favors is that the giant effigies are a work planned by a master mind, for only a skilled architect could have conceived the whole rhythmic design. According to her,

27

the unique scientific, religious, artistic, and agricultural knowledge embodied in it transcended all other compositions and reflects God's universe and its laws. Accordingly, in her view, the Glastonbury Zodiac is the creation of the initiates of the mystery school and gives us the key to the evolution of human consciousness. It is something deliberately designed to be passed on, down through the ages, to be rediscovered at the appropriate time, which presumably is now.

It is no secret that there is a pronounced tendency among the romantically inclined to connect the Zodiac builders with the refugee Atlanteans—wise men from the doomed continent who foresaw the imminent submergence and therefore moved eastward to found a new center of religion and science where the flame of knowledge could be kept alive. England was a safe place for preserving the ancient wisdom. This spiritual function of the Zodiac would not exclude its practical utility. Thus, for example, the Zodiac could have served as an agricultural calendar while also functioning as a "visual aid" in time recordings—perhaps even as a kind of computer or "teaching machine" for mankind. The members of the contemporary "Company of Avalon" like to point out that we are at the end of the Piscean cycle and moving into the new Aquarian age— the age of the more integrated man, the world-conscious man, and that is why the Zodiac is being regenerated. The rationale of this is presented in Fig. 7.

Above and beyond such relatively prosaic theories, *and because the Zodiac can best be seen only from the air,* it has been proposed that the Zodiac has some connection with *UFO's* ("flying saucers"), employed by interplanetary visitors from "outer space." This view has been advanced by Brinsley Le Poer Trench in his volume, *Men Among Mankind* (London, 1962). He tells us . . . "Britain is a remnant of Atlantis and that, prior to the sinking of Poseidonis, the 'Heavenly' half of the Human Race left the instructions to the earthly half in the shape of the colossal Zodiac in Somerset and in the Great Pyramid; the third point of the triangle being the island of Poseidonis itself; they then withdrew, leaving us to find our own fumbling way back to full recognition that we are but two halves of a whole, and that those who now 'look in on us' are brothers (albeit very advanced ones) having a look-see . . . "

This is indeed a fanciful picture, one which reminds one of Plato's myth of the "separation of the sexes," always longing for reunion.

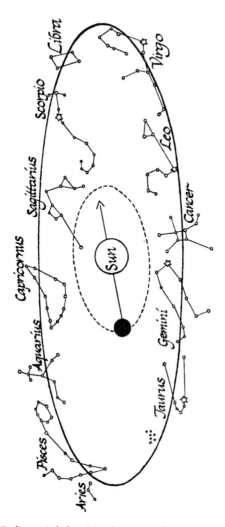

Fig. 7. The Zodiac. A belt of twelve constellations (star groups) which circle the sky close to the ecliptic, which is the plane of the earth's orbit around the sun. The sun, moon, and planets seem to move against the background of these constellations. From the earth (in this diagram) the sun seems to be in the constellation Libra. As the earth revolves, the sun will appear to move through Scorpio and Sagittarius, until finally it is back in Libra again. The Babylonians recognized this apparent motion of the sun, moon and planets. This knowledge helped the ancients predict the seasons. The Zodiac was (and is) linked to astrology, which claims to interpret the influence of the stars on people and worldly events.

Perhaps someday it will be shown how this would fit in with tne Oriental conception of the Yang-Yin complementarity!

All this meandering over the surface of the earth—and outer space too—brings one to the ultimate question: *Why was England chosen as the site of the Glastonbury Zodiac?* Here again the speculations outrun the available facts. Aside from the body of spiritual knowledge preserved by the Arcane School of Wisdom in some ethereal realm, there would have to be some material spot on the earth where the School could be incarnated, and this would have to be staffed by savants who have knowledge of things celestial and terrestrial. And here is where Avalon presents itself as the strategic spot.

Those who have studied the Somerset area have concluded that the four mounds at Cadbury, Glastonbury, Bladon, and Cardiff are exactly aligned and must have been used for signalling in the days of King Arthur and King Alfred.This may be correct; but this in itself does not explain the construction of a Zodiac 3,000 years earlier. To support the idea of the majestic role of the Glastonbury Zodiac one requires some pretty soaring views, even if the idea of "flying saucer visitors" is too far out. Moreover, as the "outsider" soon discovers, the Egyptian pyramid builders will also have to be brought into the picture. One Canadian astrologer writes as follows:

> "Using the latitude of the Great Pyramid as a base and the Pyramid's own angle, the apex would rest in England and the opposite point in the Atlantic Ocean in the supposed area of Atlantis.
>
> "Dropping the base to the tropic of Cancer, an important astrological point would bring the apex into the area of the 'Star Map.'
>
> "Using the descending passage of the Great Pyramid as a telescope, an observer in the 'Pit' would look directly at the Pole Star (then Alpha Draconis) at a certain period in the 4th millennium B.C., indicating the date of its construction.
>
> "The same condition would occur some 2,000 years later and there are indications that the original calculations were checked about 2,200 B.C. Two partitions were placed in the passage with small apertures."

These considerations, it seems, are supposed to establish the date for the Great Pyramid (Pl. VI) and the rationale of an anchor-point in England. Of course, this pyramid is one of the wonders of the ancient world. But some critics will urge that the logic for the choice

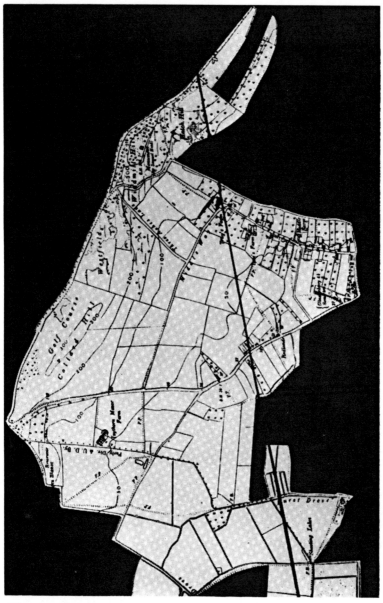

Plate V. Taurus. The line indicated shows where the equinox of 2700 B.C. would have passed through the eye of the bull and also the "bell" or "clappers", marking the place of the Royal Star Aldebaran, on the hoof at Hurst.

Plate VI. The Sphinx, with Khufu's Great Pyramid in the background.

of Glastonbury as an anchor point, a Zodiacal center, is not clear. This thesis that Egypt and England are tied together is not new. However, these considerations do broaden the problem, which then becomes: *Why Egypt?* As already noted in Trench's book, we have a three-point landing, as follows: (1) Somerset Zodiac; (2) Great Pyramid of Egypt; (3) and Poseidon (Atlantis). This kind of "triangulation" would elate all followers of Plato and could also be incorporated in Buckminster Fuller's "geodesic dome" conception— the dome in *this* case being the great earth itself.

That there is some connection, at least in the minds of the theorizers, between England and Egypt is indicated by the collateral claim that the Chalice Well of the Glastonbury center was made in accordance with measurements by the Royal Egyptian cubit. This, in turn, calls to mind the Pyramidology of Charles Piazzi Smyth, who embellished (but did not create) the theory that the Great Pyramid was built under divine guidance and incorporated cosmic units such as the "pyramid inch." This thought was put into words by one student[3] as follows:

> "Four thousand years before science discovered the line of the polar axis of the earth, the architect of the Great Pyramid used that knowledge. He also knew its precise length and used it as the master scale to determine the basic unit of measure, called the Polar Diameter Inch or the Pyramid Inch. This is the inch we use today all over the English speaking world, calling it the "British Inch."

This is a picturesque theory. But the evidence for it is not convincing. Aside from the fact that this "inch" has not been supported by measurements of the structures that supposedly embody it, the whole doctrine of a cosmic wisdom concerning the rotundity of the earth, its circumference, specific gravity and mass—all this is presupposing a reservoir of knowledge far beyond anything we presently have reasons for believing could have been possessed by any "pre-scientific" era of mankind. About the only conclusion we can draw is that if any such general confirmation is forthcoming in the future, it probably will find its main supporting evidence in the verification that the Glastonbury Zodiac is an unquestionable fact— "it is there"—and cannot be explained away as a figment of human imagination. The dimensions of the required revision of our ideas will exceed that made necessary by Professor Gerald Hawkins' studies of *Stonehenge.* Let us say a word about that.

VIII. THE ZODIAC AND STONEHENGE

Before leaving the topic of the skills and the "brains" required for building the Zodiac, one may reflect on the similar problem relative to the construction of Stonehenge. In this book, *Stonehenge Decoded* (New York, 1965), Professor Gerald Hawkins discusses this problem of how men of the Stone Age could have possessed so much scientific knowledge as the building of such structures in England and Scotland required.

England's Stonehenge is unlike any other circle of stones (Dolmen) in the world. As Henry James responded: "It stands as lonely in history as it does on the great Salisbury plain." Why is it there? What does it mean? Is it a Druid temple of the sun? A place of human sacrifice? Or as Professor Hawkins has shown (though there are those who still are unconvinced), is it a sophisticated and brilliantly conceived astronomical observatory . . . a Neolithic computer designed and used by three different groups of peoples over a 400-year period, beginning about 1,900 years B.C.?

Professor Hawkins suggests that early man in Europe was much more intelligent than generally had been thought. Indeed, his enthusiasm runs so high that he remarks in his book that it should have been dedicated: "To Stone Age man—misunderstood—underestimated." This same point has been made by Alexander Marshak; his studies on the lunations of the Upper Paleolithic period lead him to the same conclusion, i.e., that there must be a re-evaluation of the origins of human culture, including the origins of art, religion, astronomy, and other skills. Doubtless Mrs. Maltwood's findings and interpretations lead to similar conclusions, except even more so.

At this point we cannot go into further details concerning the Stonehenge circle. For present purposes it is sufficient to call attention to the Sarsen circle, the outside ring of Stonehenge, which contains the free standing upright stones, with a third stone across the top. These five trilithons within the Sarsen circle form a horseshoe and near one of these, the central trilithon, is the so-called altar stone. According to Professor Hawkins, "the where and the why of this stone are not even to be guessed at." However, the heelstone, visible through openings between the stones, does have an explanation—it was used as a sighting point. We must always keep in mind that the Stonehengers lived by the sun and the moon, and so they placed the heelstone at a spot where the sun would rise over the heelstone.

Later I shall consider the suggestion that the purpose of the altar stone was to serve as a place for the Druids to put a glass or crystal sphere or "egg" (a "burning glass") to focus the rays of the sun and start their sacred fires at the time of the winter solstice. There is something to be added to this ingenious theory, but more of that toward the conclusion of our investigations.

It is not clear what reasons Katherine Maltwood had for holding that the builders of the Zodiac were not the builders of Stonehenge, except for the postulated time gap that separates them, along with her conviction concerning the differences in skills and knowledge required by the builders of the Zodiac as compared with the Stonehengers. But her opinions were formed *before* the "decoding" of Stonehenge. When Mrs. Maltwood carried on her investigations, Professor Hawkins was unknown to the scientific community. Now all of that is changed. If the builders of Stonehenge were so incredibly clever, they, or their ancestors of 1,000 years earlier, *could have built both the Zodiac and Stonehenge!*

It may be that there would be a difference in the types of abilities required in the two foregoing cases—skills in earthworks construction and irrigation and stoneworks. But even this is not an unbridgeable difficulty. When one takes into account Avebury monuments and other constructions, one is inclined to conclude that there was a highly civilized race of Britons living in England. Indeed, there may well have existed a cosmopolitan society all over Europe, three or four thousand years before the Christian era. However that may be, it is clear that these proto-Aryans (Indo-Europeans), or refugee Atlanteans, or whoever they were, must have had a superior knowledge of geometry and astronomy, such as the Pythagoreans displayed at a later date. A possible confirmation of this is provided by Silbury Hill, about 60 miles from Glastonbury Tor, where—it has been supposed—either a Golden Calf or a Golden Horse and Rider are buried in the Hill. After reading Moses B. Cotsworth's *The Rational Almanac*, it became plausible to hold that the horse and rider are concealed in the hill and that this is related to the angles the sun makes on the Hill with the spring equinox in Taurus and the winter solstice in Sagittarius. If then, by analogy, we transpose this configuration to the Glastonbury maze—as Miss Elizabeth Leader proposes—we may think of Arthur as typifying the sun, as Hercules does in another time and place in human culture.

All this calls attention to the fact that the story is very incomplete. Much more research is called for.

PART II

The Meaning of the Tor

I. HISTORY: FROM DRUIDISM TO CHRISTIANITY

We now move to the next rung of our ladder of spiritual escalation.
From this vantage point we propose to survey the panorama of
Glastonbury Abbey and the other "early spots" associated with it.
The complete purview must inevitably include a number of things:
the Tor Hill, and a glance at the early monks of the Abbey, these
surveys being in the nature of a preparation for the study of King
Arthur and his Knights of the "Table Round." To do an adequate
job, these places and events must be set in context, and this means
a recapitulation of the relevant historical background, insofar as
this is known. I shall keep this as brief as possible, whilst not neg-
lecting significant materials.

When we begin with the Druids and Druidism, this seems like a
dubious start. In this field, as one author has put it, there has been
much of the "nonsense that luxuriates in the lunatic fringe of serious
archæology." This is possible, of course, because relatively little
authentic history is available concerning the Druids. In that case,
however, one wonders how it is possible to establish who is guilty of
"nonsense"? We can only strive to keep our "nonsense" to a mini-
mum in terms of the canons of scientific historiography. While
Druidism still survives, since the Druids hold their annual con-
claves, this residue is not of much assistance in dealing with the
historical problems.

First off, we must note that the origin of the Druids is lost in
archaic fog. Not a great deal is known of this subject. One of the
better known accounts is found in the Sixth Book of Julius Caesar's
Gallic War (*De Bella Gallia*). This account, however, comes at a
relatively late date and may not present an impression of Druidism
"at its best." Since the Druidical priesthood resisted the Roman

incursions with fanatical zeal, the Romans were forced to try to suppress them as an organized opposition. Among other things, this meant cutting down their sacred groves. The charge that the Druids practiced human sacrifice may have been an exaggeration or invention on the Roman's part for the purpose of denigrating the Druid faith. Of course, if one is going to moralize about the past, it could be noted that the Romans, on this score, were in the position of "the pot calling the kettle black"—as witness their persecutions of the early Jews and Christians.

It is not surprising that our records of the Druids are so fragmentary. Like the Bretons of Brittany, they did not commit their teachings to permanent forms, as for example the Sumerians did. It has been said, however, that the Druids did use a Greek alphabet in their writing. In any case, some relics and artefacts have survived, especially the stone circles of Druid worship. Some of these are very similar to the Sumerian and Babylonian Ziggurats (see Fig. 8 for an example of these) and this suggests a common origin. I shall return to this topic at a later stage. Meantime we note that the "end"

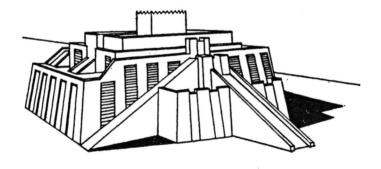

RESTORATION OF THE ZIGGURAT AT UR

Fig. 8.

of ancient Druidism—like its beginning—is difficult to date. But whatever vestiges may have survived the Roman legions were obliterated by Christianity, which absorbed some of its doctrines and ritual. This is an interesting phenomenon and will merit further attention at a later point.

Like the Celtic priests to whom the word "Druid" may be applied,

36

the origin of the word *Druid* is obscure. One theory is that the name is derived from *Drus*, the oak tree sacred to the Druids. Others hold that this verbal similarity is accidental, and they prefer an alternative theory that the word is derived from *Druthin*, a "servant of the truth." Perhaps these two suggested derivations are not mutually exclusive.

Whatever the origin of the Druids and the name applied to them, Druidism in time culminated in a religious philosophy — perhaps even a proto-science—for as Caesar says of the Druids, "they also lecture on the stars in their motion, the magnitude of the earth and its dimensions, on natural history . . ." Caesar also points out that the Druids believed their souls never die but survive beyond death. Another remarkable fact is that, even in Caesar's time, the Druids, like the Hebrew tribes of Levi, were exempt from taxes and military service.

It has been argued that Druidism can be traced back to "Hu the Mighty," who about the year 1,800 B.C. reportedly systematized mnemonically the wisdom of the ancients, a group whom he had conducted westward into Britain. Whether the mighty Hu did in fact lead the first colony of Cymri into Britain is conjectural; and even more so is the attribution to him of the building of Stonehenge. Here again we are caught up in the veil of obscurantism which covers the scene.

We have already noted that the Druids placed high value on learning and education. It is said that there were four colleges, each presided over by a chief or Archdruid. Many of the beliefs and practices apparently resembled the doctrines of the Pythagoreans and the Essenes (I shall return to this), especially the emphasis on the communal or corporate life and the reverence for learning and the traditions of astrology. Some of the "holy wells" on Druidic sites were used as telescopes, hence the maxim, "truth lies at the bottom of a well." It has even been urged that the unit of measurement in the erection of Stonehenge was the cubit, the same as used in the construction of the Great Pyramid. This does not necessarily imply that the Druids had a hand in the construction of the "observatory" on Salisbury plain—it would be sufficient if the "Stonehengers" were indoctrinated in Druidic science. However that may be, the Druids certainly built their "temples," which were circles of stones, at places cut off from their surroundings, i.e., each of these sanctuaries was a "caer." Some of the circles were monolithic constructions apparently symbolic of the sun's paths through the Zodiac; that is, the stone circles had reference to the constellations. Druidic services were held when the sun was above the horizon, and the Archdruid then occupied a central position in the enclosure.

Somewhat to our surprise, we are informed that centers of Druid worship were located at Iona and at Glastonbury. In the latter case, the Tor would serve as a marvellous spot for sun worship. According to the *Bardas*, the cosmography of the Druidic universe is described in circles, as of course the Pythagoreans also taught. It may be that the circular groves of Druidism reflected this circular-celestial cosmography, and that this, metaphorically, extended to circles of transmigrations of souls (metempsychosis).

We must be warned, however, that it may be all too easy to attribute a uniqueness to Druidism beyond what the facts may justify. In this early stage of cultural evolution a solar religion was quite generally associated with the belief in "divine kingship"—the worship of an earthly ruler ("Archdruid" among the Celts?), who reigned by divine right or "heavenly" authority. This is illustrated by King Hammurabi of Chaldea (about 1,700 B.C.), who claimed that he had received his codification of the law from the sun god. According to J. G. Frazer, this belief in a sun deity and the solar origin of kingship was shared by Aryans from India to Ireland.

At the risk of a slight digression, and in connection with these cosmological conceptions, one must at least make mention of the claim, attributed to Clement of Alexandria and others, that Gaulish Druids were the teachers of Pythagoras and members of his school. It has been argued that the Pythagorean brotherhood must have known of and assented to the Druidic teachings, so similar are the tenets. For that matter—while we are on the mental safari—one can find some notable similarities between Druidism and the Essene doctrines of the sect at Qumran. One may easily compose the syllogism:

> Pythagoras was influenced by Druidism
> The Essenes were Pythagoreans
> Therefore, the Essenes were Druidically influenced

All this, outlandish though it may seem, could have a measure of plausibility, especially if it can be shown that there was a Mediterranean culture spread about from India to Ireland, say about 5 or 4 thousand years B.C. But to be frank, this raises as many questions as it answers.

We have mentioned the centrality of Ireland. Where and when the very earliest inhabitants of Ireland originated is still unknown. When the Celts moved in the resulting civilization of Gaelic Ireland (Hibernia) became a theocratic society, the tribes unified seemingly by a common mythology concerning the Gods of Dana, a mythology which was embodied in a sacred, secret writing of Ideograms.

Druidism had a strong hold in Ireland. It is said that King Achaius (1383 B.C.) built an academy at Tara, called the "Court of the Learned." This latter was subsequently enlarged by King Carmac. There is ample evidence that there were in Ireland sacred ritual enclosures similar to the stone circles in Britain. Also the Druids in Ireland—like their counterparts in Britain—were magicians versed in oak tree lore.

The interaction between Christianity and Druidism in Ireland is a matter of considerable interest. There is little question but that Druidism in Ireland and Britain was mingled with a much older and earlier religion, "pagan" in nature. From a casual glance, the relative ease with which Druidism accepted Christianity, and vice versa, may seem a bit surprising—it is almost as if Druidism were a preparation for Christianity. The doctrinal similarities concerning survival must have helped to ease the transition. Fanciful people, especially among the Welsh, may find closer ties, for the Druidic *Jesu* is supposed in some vague way to foreshadow the Jewish Jesus, as if the Welsh Jesu personified an Archdruid for the coming Christianity. In Welsh "Jesus" is pronounced "Esse," and those who like to indulge their fancies in Celtic mysticism will connect the supposed linguistic homology with the "Essenes" of the Qumran community with whom Jesus supposedly lived as a youth.

These cultural homomorphisms are no problem for Professor Marcel F. Homet. In his book, *Sons of the Sun* (London, 1963), Professor Homet argues the case for the view that the Druids and the stone circles and zodiacs came from Atlantis. He has little difficulty in envisaging *Homo Atlanticus* as a people who wandered to all points of the compass—to use a phrase retroactively—from their home base at Atlantis, thereby becoming the progenitors of Homo sapiens, Cromagnon man, the Celts, and of course, the Druids (see Fig. 9, based on a diagram from Homet's book). Accord-

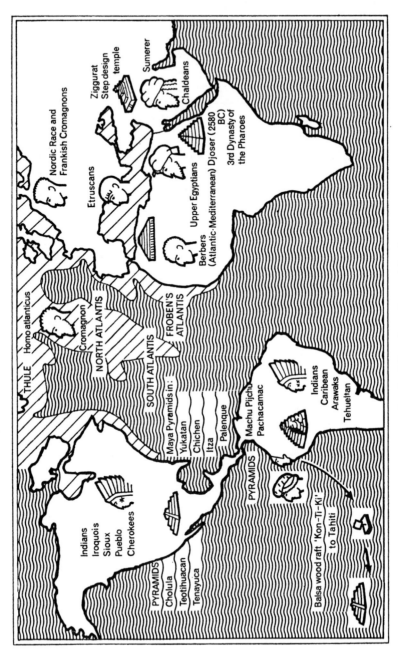

Fig. 9. Migrations from Atlantis

ingly—so Professor Homet informs us—the Druids were the descendants of the earlier eastward migrating Atlanteans who perfused their knowledge into the Celts, from Britain and Brittany to Gaul and points further East and West. This, therefore, would contain the essence of the "Hibernian mystery"—the Irish-Atlanteans who created the magnetized Isle of Eire! And this Atlantean-Iberian-Hibernian culture was then, at a later date, spread abroad when good old St. Patrick came upon the stage, properly to end his days at Avalon's Abbey—not far from King Arthur!

This marvelous cyclodrama is of course ridiculed by the flat-footed and unromantic pedants. Too, the sober geologists insist that there never was such a continent, at least not in the last one million years. For these skeptics, therefore, there is no point in discussing whether the Atlanteans could have been the forefathers of the Zodiac builders, the Pyramids, or anything else. There would be too many millennia separating the hypothetical Atlanteans from any people of recorded history or conjectured pre-history. But if Plato's time-scale is closer to the truth than that of the academic geologists (in the one direction) or the revised scale of Professor Angelos Galanopoulos and the Santorin-Thera group (in the other direction), then Plato and Homet could still be right. All things are possible—with the "right" time scales!

And so we still have our problems. Both the Glastonbury Abbey and the Avalonian Zodiac mysteries may at least have a common core. According to Bligh Bond and Mrs. Maltwood, the measurements and the design have a cosmic message; they convey a cosmic meaning, via the "canon of proportion," uniting man (microcosm) and the macrocosm.

If we grant that the effigies were in fact constructed by intelligent architects-engineers, then presumably a master mind had to conceive the whole rhythmic mosaic of the Zodiac wheel—the archetype for the *Round Table* counterpart wherein the Knights, like their heavenly "twins" of the zodiacal configurations, play out their roles in a cosmic cyclodrama. And if, perchance, we incline to believe all this is possible, does it predispose us toward the fabulous notion that the British Israelites were descendants of the original Eastward-wandering Atlanteans as the initiates who preserved and transmitted the ancient mysteries as these were later taught at Glastonbury,

41

Stonehenge, and perhaps also at Camelot? Let us proceed, and see what develops.

II. THE ABBEY AND ITS LEGENDS

The story of Avalon or Glastonbury is important for a number of reasons: because it is the place, supposedly, where Joseph of Arimathea built his first Christian church; because it is the site of some of King Arthur's exploits as well as his eventual burial spot; and finally because this is the "Second Rome" (*Roma Secunda*), the meeting place of Celt and Saxon as the center of state and church interactions, the source of mystical Grail legends, and the well-spring of English medieval and later civilization. Beyond all that, as we have seen, it is the home of the "Temple of the Stars," the celestial lamp which may illuminate the mystery play of the ages, posing a problem which students now discern but have not been able to solve.

In this survey we can only sketch some of the high points in this panoramic view. The details of the pageant must be gleaned from the more exhaustive studies, when they are available. Some of the highlights have already been described. In addition, we still have before us the story of King Arthur and the Zodiac. Much of this revolves around Avalon, and we are not finished with the episodes which have their center in this area. A few comments, here and there, may prove helpful in clarifying the sequence of events in this forward moving story.

In its earliest era Glastonbury had been named *Ynnis-Witrin,* the crystal or glassy isle; then in following periods it was also named Isle of Avilion, Avalon, and finally Glastonbury. This baptismal Odyssey did not exclude the claim that the Isle of Avalon was related by name to Avallach, a primeval Celtic demigod who purportedly presided over the Underworld, a mysterious place of rendezvous for the dead. It was to this glassy island, perhaps by way of a glassy boat, that Arthur was transported, there to be healed of his wounds and to be ready for his "second coming."

Approaching material somewhat less mythological in nature, we know that the people of Britain were among the first to accept Christianity, Glastonbury thereby earning the title of the "mother church" of England. It is to be noted, however, that the precise date for this —whether 37 A.D. or 63 A.D.—is not established. In either case,

Glastonbury was the seat of the first Christian church in Britain and England the first nation to accept this religion, this perhaps because of an inbuilt disposition of Britons toward a "magnetic induction" operating between Druidism and Christianity.

However that may be, it is clear that even before the arrival of the monks at Glastonbury, there was an aura of the mysterious and the supernatural surrounding the site of Glastonbury. Apparently from the outset Avalon was destined to become something more than, or different from, the hill-forts erected by the Celts. We need always to keep in mind the role of pagan as well as Christian supernaturalism which runs like an Ariadne's thread through the labyrinthine pattern of Glastonbury, a thread which appears in three successive tapestries on the loom of time.

The Growth of Maryology

Religious historians of the romantic cast like to play with the idea that St. Mary lies buried in Avalon. In his book, *St. Joseph of Arimathea at Glastonbury*, the Rev. Lionel S. Lewis devotes an entire Appendix to this topic. By the time the Knights had gathered around the Round Table, devotion to the legend of the Madonna—the Blessed Virgin—was well established. As noted, the Glastonbury monks had established a prototype for Maryology by enshrining the Virgin at the very heart of the Glastonbury traditions. The monasticism of the monks exalted chastity as a virtue. Small wonder, then, that when Queen Guinevere violates her vow of fidelity, her faithlessness appears as a grievous sin in the eyes of the Arthurian court. The "Virgin Mary" theme does not lose its dominance until the time of Henry VIII, when many and various changes were the order of the day.

The Norman chapel of St. Mary was built in 1184, after the great fire, at which time the remains of St. Patrick were placed in a pyramid south of the altar of St. Mary's chapel (for a picture of this, see the Rev. Lewis's book, page 79). True, one may question the historicity of the reports of these providential events, but it is entirely possible that St. Patrick, being a Briton by birth, should return to his native land to be buried there.

The ideological significance of all this is not obvious unless one is thinking of the possibility of a present-day ecumenical movement in England comparable to that which has taken place in Rome in

43

recent years. That there should once more be a united Christian church in England is not impossible, though of this no one (to my knowledge) has found any prognostication in the Somerset Zodiac. How *could* there be such a prophecy? In general, there are too many lacunae in the script to discern any one single drama being enacted. Among the discontinuities are the following: In the first place, the Glastonbury monks show no knowledge of the Zodiac. But then, one wonders, why should they? They were occupied with church and chapel and the Zodiac did not exist for them, or if it did, it was part of the heathen past. Why then, if and when the monks (or their departed spirits) established paranormal contact through Bligh Bond's medium, should they say anything about the Zodiac and its builders?

In the second place, Mrs. Maltwood shows no knowledge of Bligh Bond's *Gate of Remembrance*. It will be recalled that the Glastonbury Abbey was excavated by Bligh Bond and when he could not get enough information about the Edgar and Loretto chapels through accepted archæological procedures, he resorted to paranormal procedures. The "results" have been much disputed and his methods widely questioned. As we have already noted, Mrs. Maltwood says little about the Abbey, and still less about Mr. Bond's spiritistic excursions. One exception to the former occurs in her book, *The Enchantments of Britain*, where Katherine Maltwood says:

"What the Phoenix will bring forth in her anguish during the next two thousand years that the sun inhabits its sacred precincts Time only will prove. Can the fine old Abbey be restored in which to worship the Great Architect of the Universe? Can the little town of Glastonbury be cleansed by the waters of its once holy 'Chalice Well,' (the Aquarian Cup) from the miasma of pseudo-occultism? Can it by strictly scientific investigation of the 'Ancient Wisdom,' rise on the wings of the 'Evangelistic Eagle' soaring into the gold and azure of a new sunrise, the clouds of which are even now like a furnace of molten copper.

"Up, up the long delirious burning blue
Where never lark or even eagle flew
Behold the day cometh that shall burn as an oven—
But unto you who fear my name shall the Sun of
Righteousness arise with healing in His wings."

(*Malachi*, IV. 2)

44

There is prophecy enough in this passage. There are also anxious questions. In her own form of circumspection, Mrs. Maltwood observes that in some of the old Somerset churches one may find old carvings of the Zodiac animals, and this only confirms her thesis: whether it was the Cauldron of Ceridwen, the Ocean of Knowledge, the Chalice, or the Holy Grail, it was the Zodiac that the true Initiates had in mind. These reflections remind one of another prophetic passage, this time in William Malmesbury's *Antiquities of Glastonbury*, where he hints at "some sacred secret" sealed under the floor of St. Mary's chapel, and one is supposed to be able to discover the intimations of this mighty secret in the geometrical pattern of the sanctuary's mosaic, a message sealed under the floor. One wonders:

What can this mighty secret be?

To find the answer, we must probe deeper. To do this, we must enter upon what looks like another digression, though in fact it is not—as will appear subsequently.

III. IONA, GLASTONBURY, AND ST. COLUMBA

The reader may well wonder why at this point we interpolate a section on Iona and St. Columba. A fair question! There are several reasons for this, the first being an interest in the manner in which these two—Iona and St. Columba—illustrate the interaction of Celtic-Druidic paganism and Christianity in an emerging synthesis. Both components are somehow involved in the proliferation of the meaning, if the Zodiac is to have any overarching impact in history. The other reason is more difficult to explain. Later on I shall consider the "Iona current" (previously mentioned in my references to the *World Sensorium* article) which is pictured as a kind of ionizing radiation belt for mental-social evolution. For the explanation of this psycho-physical parallel we need to familiarize ourselves with some novel concepts and language of discourse. We surmise that there may be something like "planetary triangles" at work here, especially if we are to regard our earth as comparable to a "geodesic dome," that is capable of creating wholistic or configurational effects. In other words, we may have here in the "Iona current" one contribution to the *magnetic moments* effect that has been postulated in order to construct our philosophy of history.

Now to turn to St. Columba.

The available biographical facts about St. Columba are a bit scanty. The classic biography of him is by another saint. St. Adamnan's biography of St. Columba is a document filled with the accounts of the miracles and prophecies attributed to St. Columba. St. Columba, an Irish Scot, was born in the year 522 A.D. He was descended of a royal line in Ireland. It was there, in his native land, that he entered a monastery, eventually to become a monk. In the course of his life he founded many monasteries, including the monastery at Kells in Ireland, renowned for its Book of Kells. Let us pause for a moment to consider this area.

It is believed that the monastery of Kells was originally founded to house relics brought from Iona because of the Viking raids on the latter. Reaching further back into the past, it is interesting to recall that in a much earlier age (about 2,100 B.C.) the Passage Grave in the Mound of Hostages at Tara (not far from Kells) was built on the site of a pagan cemetery—so at least the authors of the *New Grange* inform us. New religions from old!

And while we are on this detour, let us also note that even though the spiral patterns of the New Grange in Ireland were inspired by Mycenaean art forms, in general the art of the Boyne tombs in Ireland reflects an earlier pre-Mycenaean civilization, one that flourished in Troy, Crete, Malta, and Iberia. This point is brought out by the authors of the *New Grange* (pp. 129-130). To a limited degree this tends to support the chronology of the Maltwood hypothesis.

Returning to Iona, we learn that in earlier times a great college of Druids flourished there. St. Columba founded the community of Iona, and here the "Soldiers of Christ" converted many pagans. According to William of Malmesbury, the princely Columba of Iona was at once preacher, poet, artist, and great organizer. Inevitably he journeyed to Glastonbury—the "Second Rome"—and there, in due time, he departed this world, this in the year 597 A.D. According to one tradition, he is buried in Glastonbury, not far from St. David (of Wales) and St. Patrick.

From this it is clear that the life story of St. Columba is captivating. One contemporary student writes me as follows:

"I have always been thrilled by the story of Iona and St. Columba, from the moment he stole the missal from the monastery in Ireland to his arrival at the Holy Isle of Iona —exiled from Ireland—and his life thereafter, not to mention the ancient prophecy, which has come so marvelously true today."

The prophecy referred to above relates to the coming events on the little Isle. As St. Columba foresaw, Iona, like Glastonbury, was destined to fall upon evil times—decay into ruins, in fact—but in the course of time it would be restored. Today those "of the faith" believe that both Iona and Glastonbury have become "sacred centers" and will progressively assume their places at the forefront of time's caravan, i.e., as places where what-was-once, and what-will-be, shall join hands. People of all nations and all religions are already journeying to these two spots for worship. And they inquire: is this not the ideal, the message of the New Age? This means the breaking down of barriers, the restoration of a simplicity in daily living, a realization that all life is One Life—an attitude to show forth in the church, the university, in shops, offices, farms, and on the high seas, wherever men live and travel. Thus the spirit will be reborn in all men, a light awaiting only the chance to shine.

As preserved in St. Adamnan's book, this is the prophecy that St. Columba uttered before his death:

"In Iona of my heart, Iona of my love
Instead of monk's voices shall be the lowing of cattle;
But ere the world comes to an end
Iona shall be as it was."

Today stone masons, carpenters, musicians, professors, fishermen, ministers—persons from all walks of life—are returning to Iona, there to worship and work and pray. Is this in some sense a confirmation of the prophecy of St. Columba, and even more, a glimpse into the future, when the old saying, "Christ will come again upon Iona," will be fulfilled?

Is there more to the prophecy? Is it possible that just as the Stone of Scone has gone from Iona to Westminster Abbey to serve as a symbol of British unity, so the stones of the Avalonian Zodiac and the Stone circle of Stonehenge will yield their "bits" to the electronic computers of our present science-oriented society to declare an ancient wisdom-religion, informing the world of a once-and-future-mightier kingdom of the spirit? Or is this merely honeymoonish dreamery? Perhaps to answer this we must fly higher, rather than "probe deeper." Let us try that excursion.

IV. TOR HILL AND THE CRETAN LABYRINTH

Early in 1967 another link in the Glastonbury chain was placed in my hands. The donor of the gift is Mr. G. N. Russell of County

47

Cork, Ireland. In the letters and documents that he has sent me, Mr. Russell affirms his belief that he has identified the legendary Holy Grail. As a result of several years of research into the labyrinth motif, Mr. Russell is convinced that the Grail is connected with the mazes which occur all over England, and that the Grail and the Cretan labyrinth are one and the same.

According to our amateur scientist, in July, 1966, while ascending the Tor Hill, he suddenly realized that he was walking on the "Grail"! That is to say, the Grail in reality is the ritual pattern of the seven terraced spiritual (spiral) paths which encircle Tor Hill; these paths are the still visible signs of the impressive proto-Druidical processions to the top of the hill to worship the sun!

True, only traces of the terraces are visible to those who are unfamiliar with sophisticated patterns. (see Fig. 10, The Pathway of the Labyrinth). To such, these would be merely sheep tracks. But Mr. Russell states that photographs reveal that the labyrinth *is* the Tor. This discovery seems to be quite unrelated to Katherine Maltwood's picture of the Zodiac; but the Tor is only a small part of the giant Zodiac and further study may reveal that the two are complementary aspects of one vast engineering project.

According to his own account, Mr. Russell's interest in this puzzle was first aroused when, in the rocky valley near Tintagel, in Cornwall, replicas of the maze motif were found. Further study of the interlacing spirals soon revealed that the labyrinth is the basis of a game, sometimes referred to as "troy" or "troytown." As a "game" played on Tor Hill, it is followed by circumambulating the terraced rings around the hill in an order numbering from the bottom, 3, 2, 1, 4, 7, 6, 5, reversing direction clockwise-anti-clockwise, seven times.

This is a most "amazing" game, a game of psychic significance and cosmic import. In the first case, the interpretation fits in with the "Grail" as the container of psychic energy which Carl Jung visualized as being a constant movement between two poles within the psyche—sometimes called Heaven and Hell. As a cosmic symbol, the interlacing spirals remind one of galactic configurations. And as Mr. Russell insists, the analogue of the pattern of concentric circles all intertwined is found in Plato's *Atlantis* and in Thomas Campanella's *City of the Sun* and Stonehenge II.

Not content with linking the Tor spiral paths with the Cretan

48

The Pathway
(OF THE CRETAN LABYRINTH)

Fig. 10.

labyrinth, the Holy Grail, the Glastonbury Tor as a solar temple, or Holy Mountain as the center of a solar cult, the carved labyrinth in the Rocky Valley near Tintagel, and associating the pattern with the meaning of Stonehenge, Mr. Russell takes another leap into the dark by transposing the labyrinth to man himself. He finds that it is the *mandala*, an ancient mystic symbol of the universe as well as the representation of the convolutions of the cerebral hemispheres! We have mentioned the homomorphism which Mr. Russell believes can be detected between the labyrinth and the mandalas. Down through the centuries mandalas have figured in many of the world's cultures. They have been given different interpretations in different contexts. In ancient Sanskrit they were magic circles of life—symbolic of the unity of man and the universe. In modern theories of psychiatry they would be regarded as symbols of the riddles of man in a perplexing world; this, once more, is the search for the harmony of the individual with the totality of the universe.

All this one finds in Mr. Russell's plea for a synthesis of the knowledge of the ages. Like Mrs. Maltwood, he has written to the experts for advice and assistance. They have all rebuffed him. And so he now comes to the student of philosophy. One wonders: is it possible that the labyrinth will turn out to be the morphogenetic field pattern for the embryogenesis of the *World Sensorium*? This would be a strange denouement, the likes of which has never been seen before in human history. If so, the "Zodiac" and the "labyrinth" will have to be integrated in some manner.

One of the unexpected things in his report is Mr. Russell's statement that, at the early stage, he was ignorant of Mrs. Maltwood's research into the Zodiac effigies—just as she, in turn, was not informed of, or more probably disregarded, Bligh Bond's use of spiritism as a hoped-for technique in finding knowledge. Now it is obvious that Mr. Russell is eager to correct his own limitations on this score.

The difficulty we face at this point can be put into the form of a simple question: *How is it possible, at one and the same time, for the Tor Hill to be Mrs. Maltwood's "Phoenix" and Mr. Russell's "labyrinth"?* Perhaps it is not possible "at one and the same time," but if we date the Zodiac at 2,700 B.C., we may then date the labyrinth at some later time. Whether the two sets of designers of the two different patterns knew of each other's work would be the next question. Perhaps there may be a continuity of meaning and purpose in the two "effigies," especially if both groups of architects-engineers were participants in the common ideology of what may be termed a "cosmic humanism."

In my own efforts at formulating some conclusions, I return constantly to the question of the Maltwood dating and the related question of the supposed role of the Sumerians in the construction of the Zodiac. In the long stretch of time between 3,500 and 2,000 B.C., the Sumerians represented the dominant cultural influence in the entire Near East, as Samuel Noah Kramer points out in his volume, *Sumerian Mythology* (Harper Torchbooks). These Sumerians were a non-Semitic, non-Indo-European people. They seem to have sprung up like Topsy. They perfected the cuneiform system of writing, a full-blown pantheon, and created a literature rich in content with strong spiritual overtones. But by the third millennium B.C. Sumer had ceased to exist as a political entity and Sumerian became a dead language, replaced by the Semitic Akkadian language of the people who conquered them.

This, however, raises problems for the Maltwood hypothesis of the Sumerland (Sumer) origin of the Somerset Zodiac. If the Zodiac was constructed about 2,700 B.C., the Sumerian-Phoenician people who allegedly journeyed to England should have left their homeland by 3,000 B.C., and they presumably should have taken their cuneiform writing with them. But there is no evidence that this is the case. Why was there no writing by the British Zodiac builders? In the case of the Celtic Druids, this supposedly was the result of the deliberate secret transmission of the mystery teachings. Can something like that have happened with the builders of the giant effigies? But for that matter, we don't have writings concerning Arthurian stories contemporaneous with the alleged events. Perhaps in time archæological diggings will uncover such artefacts. Meantime, we cannot regard the matter as settled. Who knows what else lies in store for us?

V.   BLIGH BOND'S PSYCHICAL INVESTIGATIONS

One of the most curious lines of research into the Glastonbury saga is that initiated by Frederick Bligh Bond. Mr. Bond was a British architect who at first, and as Director of Excavations, employed orthodox methods of investigation. But Mr. Bond was also interested in psychical research and next resorted to spiritistic procedure, using automatic writing via a medium to record the transmitted messages. Over a period of years (from 1907 to 1911 in the first instance) these extraordinary procedures yielded about 50 communications. The literary form of the messages, purporting to come from the spirit of the monks of the Abbey, were a curious patchwork of Low Latin, Middle English, and Modern English. The proffered explanation of this mixture was that the intelligent source of the messages was a mind that was plastic to records—as was illustrated in the Gift of Tongues at the Pentecost.

The results of Bligh Bond's investigations—spurious or bona fide —were presented in Bond's unique volume, *The Gate of Remembrance* (London, 1921). Obviously, these spiritualistic methods of trying to draw upon memories of supernormal origins gave his "findings" (the Edgar Chapel, for example) a "crackpot" character in the eyes of sober scientists. For this and other reasons the Glastonbury saga has become the center of contention between factions. Later on Bond returned to his spiritualistic research and the new results were reported in a second volume, *The Hill of Vision*.

Among the communications that were received, there is one that is quite remarkable. The following passage was recorded in a "message" dated Feburary, 1918:

"The flow of spiritual forces is westward, following and impelling the forces of material things. By a law of revolution reinforced from all points in the spiritual universe, this movement is universal. This being so, the material things first appear, working on a motive very often in itself most mundane and from your point of view most unspiritual. Thus they whose habitation was in *Crete*, revisiting the memories and traditions of others of the same race and civilisation which long before had been impelled westward beyond the great continents of America to the shores of Asia, and then onwards through the desolate tracts of Asia to the great Mediterranean basin, still continued the interminable route ever westward beyond the gates of Hercules to the islands where the fire-drawn metals be . . . But soon the spiritual forces which developed and sustained this immigration had deeper objects in view. They followed and transformed it by removing mundane influences and a great spiritual development arose in the places in which their instruments had prepared the soil.

"Phocis of the race of Crete trading with Poseidon and seeking Tyrian purple was thus brought in contact with them who worshipped the One God in contra-distinction to the many . . .Thus paved the way for the building of a Temple in his settlement of *Tintagella* . . . Thus first arose that measurement and design which were afterwards as accurately reproduced by that further advance which culminated in the temple of Glastonbury. And Tintagella was the ancient place of the shrine of the High God. So the *temple,* a reproduction accurate in every measurement, was reproduced at Glaston on this foundation."

This purported spiritistic reproduction appears on page 107 of the *Gate.* The question inevitably arises: could this mention of the "Temple in the settlement of Tintagella," which "was reproduced at Glaston on this foundation" be a reference to Glastonbury's "Temple of the Stars"? *This before Mrs. Maltwood discovered the "Temple" (Zodiac)?* If so, does this—if authentic—tend to confirm Mrs. Maltwood's ideas about the Zodiac and correlative notion of Atlantis (Poseidon) as the ultimate source of the plan? And what does this passage from "the royal traveller" mean: "Phocis of the race of Crete trading with Poseidon . . . who paved the way . . ."? The entire passage bears study.

Today the field of parapsychology is more respectable than it was decades ago. But are serious students ready to accept the "word" of the Abbey monks, supposedly long since passed over to Anwen or Paradise, Iona or Horeb? For my part, it seems that if one can accept the Zodiac as what Katherine Maltwood said it was and is, one should not boggle at accepting the word of medieval spirits who speak from beyond the grave. I intend this seriously.

The reference above to "Anwen" and "paradise" is not accidental, for at this point it serves to introduce our next theme, namely, the Arcane tradition in the Glastonbury story.

VI. THE ARCANE TRADITION

Glastonbury Tor: Is it Phoenix of the Zodiac, the Cretan Labyrinth on a hill in Britain, or is it the British analogue of the Old Testament's Mount Tabor? We cannot properly rule out any of these, especially when we recall the legend that Joseph came in a ship of Tarshish to the summer-land and sojourned at a place called Paradise (a part of Glastonbury is still called "Paradise"). This bit of pre-history is recalled by the Rev. L. S. Lewis in his book on *St. Joseph*, and he links this up with the theme of immortality, for as he notes, "It must not be forgotten that Avalon was earlier Avilion, the Isle of Departed Spirits, and so might be called the British Vale of Jehosaphat" (p. 70). This legend seemingly is regarded as a racial memory of the Celtic days of Avilion when the spirits of the departed were supposed to pass through the Tor.

This reminiscence reminds us of what, for want of a better term, may be called the "underworld" of occultism, and gives us one more theory about the Glastonbury saga. Hints of such superphysical speculations appear in the writing of Eduard Schuré, Lewis Spence, Eleanor Merry, Bligh Bond, and Mary Caine. I shall do my best to summarize this line of thought, since I am attempting to provide a complete picture.

The views of Eleanor Merry are very similar to the conceptions of Rudolf Steiner and we cannot pursue that philosophy here. It is sufficient to say that her world-view as outlined in the book *The Flaming Door* (1962), emphasizes the element in the original Hibernian mysteries—the doctrine of *Anwen*, the *Underworld*, which had to be passed through in experience before the higher spiritual world could be known. This is the so-called plunge into the Depths, an astral Hell and Heaven conception.

The best general exposition of this line of thought that I have found appears in Lewis Spence's book, *The Mysteries of Britain*. In his chapter on "The Arcane Tradition," we are informed about Anwen, the underworld "astral plane," portrayed as Hades, to which Arthur must descend in order to seize the cauldron of mystical inspiration (Spence's book has a picture of this on page 123). In presenting this interpretation, Spence is following Taliesen and the Welsh Bards. The quest of Arthur and his Knights for the miraculous is therefore really a search for the "cup of wisdom" (*Caer Sidi*, which sometimes means Zodiac), and this is the genesis of the Holy Grail of the later Christian version. The Knights of the Round Table seek the cauldron by way of a glass boat (crystal ball?); or perhaps they journey to a Glass Castle or Glass Island? We cannot say definitely.

It has also been suggested that this astral or arcane function of the "cauldron" was entangled with the theme of initiation rites performed on the Tor, perhaps even a reflection of some supposed connection with the powers of fertility, as Mrs. Mary Caine has surmised. Witchcraft could also have played a role here.

Arcane Interpretations

And now, to make the transition to theosophical interpretations somewhat tighter, let us remind ourselves again that the world-system of the Druids was based on astrological ideas fused with notions of metempsychosis ("reincarnation") and the secret wisdom of the wisdom cults. The resemblance of Druid to Pythagorean doctrine has already been mentioned. This is recognized in the scholarly volume, *King Arthur's Avalon*, by Geoffrey Ashe (1963), a work more sober and judicious than that of the Reverend Lewis.

As an example of cosmic components, one may note that the two vertical stones of the Druid Trilithons—two vertical stones united by a covering horizontal stone—resemble the horns of the celestial bull as representing two great cosmic forces, separated but united by the universal power of the sun or the spiritual world. This brings us to Eduard Schuré and his theosophical or Rosicrucian interpretations.

The present author made use of Schuré's version of the "cosmic forces" in the volume on *Cosmic Humanism*, this in connection with the problem of Jesus and the Dead Sea Scrolls. In an eloquent passage, Schuré draws this analogy:

"Sometimes in mid-Atlantic, the wind tears a rent in the cloudy sky, and one sees the clouds gather at one spot and drop towards the ocean in the shape of a horn. At the same time the sea rises up in a peak, to meet the clouds. It seems as though the whole mass of waters rushes to this liquid whirlpool, to be swirled about and caught up in it. Suddenly the two points, attracting one another, meet like two mouths. The waterspout is formed! The wind sucks up the sea, and the sea drinks the wind. A living column, vortex of air and water, moves giddily above the tossing waves, and for a moment earth and sky are united.

"The manifestation of Christ, descending from the spiritual world, through the astral and etheric planes, to the physical, resembles this marine phenomenon. In both cases, the powers of heaven and earth are at work, collaborating to bring about a supreme union. But while the waterspout is formed in a few minutes by the violence of the tempest and the electrical currents, the descent of the Christ to earth requires thousands of years, and has its primal cause in the arcana of our planetary system."

This passage is quoted from Schuré's book, *From Sphinx to Christ* (page 227). This is the basis for a further development of the theme, which runs as follows:

> "There are two psychic currents that envelop the earth with their multiple rings, like ever-moving serpents of electricity. The one that Moses named *Horeb,* and Orpheus Erebus, can also be called the contripetal force. It has its center in the earth, and draws back to her everything that falls into its torrential flood . . .The other current is named Iona by Moses, and can also be called the *centrifugal force.* It contains the forces of expansion, as the other contains those of contraction; and it is linked with the whole Cosmos. It enables souls to rise again to the sun and to heaven; it is the vehicle of divine influences; and it is by means of it that Christ descended in the symbol of the Dove. But although initiates, prepared through a long evolution for their cosmic voyage, knew in all ages how to enter the current of Iona after their death, the great mass of souls, still blinded by the darkness of matter, could accomplish this only with difficulty, and often scarcely merged from the current of Horeb between their incarnations."

As previously pointed out in my "World Sensorium" article, this line of thought can be connected with the idea of a *Psi*-layer as a medium for parapsychological phenomena. This layer or field is the medium for the "radiation belts of thought." I shall return to this; for the moment, let us stick to our job as the expositor of the ideas of others about this intriguing topic.

The one student whose views come closest to those of Schuré as just presented is Mrs. Mary Caine, a British investigator whose ideas are still in process of formulation. At the moment, I do not have the full story of Mrs. Caine's reconstruction of the Zodiac story. But for her, too, *Iona* is more than an island—it is connected with Lingam and Yoni, which appears in other systems in the picture Yang and Yin as interacting forces playing between earth and sun. Mrs. Caine ventures further and regards these cosmic forces as assisting in the formation of the giant effigies which therefore can not be entirely man-made. Her view requires that Iona be envisaged in a manner reminiscent of Eduard Schuré; but this part of the story is still her secret, to be revealed when her book on the Zodiac is out.

As Mrs. Caine sees it (through the eyes of a dubious etymology, some critics will insist), the word *Iona* is the concealed name of God (Job, Yahweh, Jove, Jonan, etc.), i.e., creation by a self-sacrificing god, with the ancient mystery of super-sex as the insemination of inchoate matter by Spirit. Here, of course, "sex" is not the animalistic drive of Freudian psychiatry—it is the Divine Energy which dives into the sea—a "water mystery," in short—and then emerges clothed in matter to come forth and prophesy. This Divine inspiration enters the earth's atmosphere from outer space. In the Zodiac of Avalon the symbol of the Dove is the source of the rays which emanate from the beak of the Dove.

St. Columba came into the kaleidoscopic pageant when he colonized Iona, an island sacred to the Druids. His name is not accidental. According to Mrs. Caine, Columba derives from Column in Greek, which leads her to Schuré's waterspout parable —a continuous column between sea and sky. The Tower of Babel, like ziggurats in Babylonia, was an attempt to restore this connection between heaven and earth by means of a pyramid or tower (Tor).

As we have seen, there have been a number of conceptions of the Holy Grail. The Grail has been connected with the Tarot cards; in hermetic script, we are assured, the Grail represents the dive into the cup to find the essential wisdom. And now the Grail has some conjunction with the Tower of Babel. According to Mrs. Caine's interpretation, the Tower of Babel appears as a kind of umbilical cord passing from Heaven to Earth. As already noted, this supposedly harks back to the original meaning of colomen as a pillar or tower. The German word for dove is *Taube* (related to *tauchen*, to dive), while the *D* of *Dove* means dot in primitive Celtic, hence Dolmen—the door between heaven and earth. This, it is said, is the "mystery of Iona"—God (Logos) made Flesh.

The fable of Arthur's descent into *Anwen* in a glass boat seems to enshrine a mnemonic mystery rite of the unconscious, the Ionic descent of the *Anwen Dove* into matter, comparable, Mrs. Caine says, to my own theory of the spiral electromagnetic action downward and upward again.

How is that for an integration of knowledge? Are we on the

57

right track? If this is so, and to get to the end of the trail, we needs must return to Arthur and see how he fits into this maze-like pattern. How may the labyrinthine adventures of the Arthurian Knights of the Round Table help to complete the puzzle picture of the Zodiac?

PART III

Camelot, King Arthur, and the Grail

I. THE MEANING OF ARTHUR

Camelot, a city of shadowy palaces
And Stately, rich in emblem and the work
Of ancient kings who did their days in stone.
—Alfred Lord Tennyson.

In the above lines the poet Tennyson provides the setting for the noble King Arthur—Camelot's "eternal hero"—the master of Cadbury Castle, a temple whose walls and battlements glitter like jewels in the ethereal mists of legends and folklore. According to one legend, Arthur came out of the seas, conquered on land, and is now everlastingly "in the air."

Who, then, was Arthur? A piltdown chieftain? A culture hero? The Egyptian Osiris embodied in a western incarnation? The supernatural "Wild Huntsman"? An avatar of Druidism? A Celtic messiah? Or only a West Country general, lord of Cadbury castle? Whatever the answer, it is clear that Arthurian legends have taken on messianic overtones. But how much is sheer mythology and how much is verified fact? For example, was there ever a Merlin's Cave at Tintagel?

Today there is established in England the Camelot Research Committee, an archæological body headed by Sir Mortimer Wheeler, renowned as the excavator of Mohenjo-Daro and the Indus civilization. In Somerset, the West Country of England, this group is digging to uncover the verities—if any—concerning Tennyson's:

> *... gray king whose name, a ghost*
> *streams like a cloud, man-shaped*
> *from mountain peak*
> *And cleaves to cairn and cromlech ...*

59

Will they find at Camelot (See Plate VII) the evidences of legends confirmed?

About Arthur this much of legend seems to be accepted. The British chieftan was the son of Uther, called "Pendragon" (chief or head). He probably was a prince of a tribe of Britons in South Wales who came to sovereignty about 510 A.D. Arthur overcame the Saxons in twelve battles, and as the central figure in many victories gained much affection and reverence from the populace.

Arthur reigned in peace for about 20 years, until his nephew Modred revolted. After being grievously wounded in the battle of Camlon, he was taken to Glastonbury where he died and was buried. His grave supposedly was opened about 1150 (facts are uncertain), and there the Monarch's bones and sword were found. Upon the cross marking Arthur's grave are inscribed the words:

"Here lies buried the famous King Arthur in the land of Avalonia."

Stories about Arthur's prowess have been told and retold over the centuries. He was endowed with every virtue. The legends are endless. Almost equally famous are the Knights of the *Round Table*. Sir Galahad, Sir Lancelot, and the others, defended honour against evil and persevered in the quest for the Holy Grail.

Arthur's birth and death have an air of mystery about them. One story tells of his arrival as an infant when he came from the sea, riding on a great wave. Miracles also attended his coronation. In the "last great battle of the West," Arthur was wounded and carried away; but the prophecy proclaimed that "he cannot die," and will return. One of the best known of Arthur's exploits is enshrined in the fable of the king of Somerset who kidnapped Guinevere and imprisoned her on Glastonbury Tor, this spot then to be besieged by King Arthur and his Knights who, working from the operational base at Camelot, and with the help of the forces of Cornwall, rescued Lady Guinevere.

As all lovers of Arthurian lore know only too well, the adulterous love of Queen Guinevere for Lancelot is the betrayal which breaks the fellowship of the Round Table, so that Modred, the scheming nephew of Arthur, could then plot the death of Arthur. In psychic motivation this act of adultery resembles the betrayal of Judas and the "kiss of death."

As we have noted, Arthur supposedly was buried near St. Joseph at Glastonbury Abbey. Later the body of Queen Guinevere, his wife, was brought from Amesbury to rest by Arthur's side. There they remained together, so legend tells us, until they were reburied in a giant oak tomb, by order of King Henry II. The Queen, it was said, had a mass of golden hair wrapped in a turban—hair that disintegrated when touched by the sun and air.

II. GRAIL LEGENDS AND THE KNIGHTS

At the time of King Arthur, in the sixth century, chivalry in its medieval forms, was still unknown in Britain. The term "chevalerie" denotes a Norman derivation and influence dating to the 11th century and the subsequent epoch. By this time the earlier tales had been further embellished. Following Mallory's *Morte d' Arthur*, these tales were glamorized by the stories of the quest for the Holy Grail—a British crusade associated with the saintly knights, Perceval (the *Parsifal* of Wagner), or Sir Galahad in other versions. This is the picturesque age of chivalry, when "knighthood was in flower," creating themes for the singers of ballads who recounted the marvelous deeds in the courts and castles throughout Europe.

The very sound of the names, Camelot, Avalon, Merlin, Sir Galahad, Guinevere, Arthur—all carry a certain magic, a magic which, in the words of one author, "sighs like a wandering wind through the forest of Arthurian and Druid legends." And as Eleanor Merry puts it, consciously or unconsciously, we are crying out for the return of Arthur and the Wisdom of the Holy Grail.

King Arthur, of course, had a great deal "going for him" as a military and culture hero. But when the religious themes were combined with magic and millennialism, an irresistible potion was served up for the incurably romantic. Reverie, legend, and nostalgia conspired in the laminated image-building of Arthur. History was transfigured when it was perfused with mysticism to suggest that the Holy Grail was buried under the Chalice Well, its waters blood red like the drops of Christ's blood in the precious cup that St. Joseph brought to Britain, following the crucifixion of Christ on Calvary. Like Arthur's sword Excalibur, some legend or other was always available to be resurrected to rekindle the sinking flames of enthusiasm and missionary zeal. In the same way, Arthur's grave—empty or not—will always provide inspiration for generations still unborn. The remains of the once magnificent Abbey (see Fig. 4, p. 18) have been reconstructed by architects, and give some idea of its grandeur.

As if all this religiosity were not enough, it is claimed that King Arthur was descended of St. Joseph; while St. David has also been reputed to be the uncle of King Arthur. Assuredly a noble ancestry! In the Reverend Lionel Lewis's book on *St. Joseph* (p. 159) this storied line of descent is traced. Aside from that, it has also recently been claimed that the list of Argonauts in Robert Graves's book, *The White Goddess,* corresponds very closely to the lists of the Knights of the Round Table. If this be true, it can hardly be an accident—statistically well nigh impossible. This, in turn, reminds one of the attempt to establish some connection between the Old Testament "sons of Jacob," and the figures in ancient Greek mythology. These "family trees" are all part of the complicated problems.

There appears to be no reason why the Knights of the Round Table should not be given names that correspond to those of the sons of Jacob, or that these names should correspond to those of the figures of Greek Mythology—at least on the assumption of a cosmopolitan civilization spread over Europe and the Near East. What would be more exciting would be the establishment of a general principle that whenever we have a teacher and twelve disciples, we have reason to conjecture that there is in operation here a principle of "signatures"; i.e., earthly counterparts of the sun and the signs of the Zodiac—all illustrated in their reincarnation in Joseph and the coat of many colours, the twelve Apostles of Christ, King Arthur's Twelve Knights, the twelve Gates of the New Jerusalem, and so on. But all of these, in the eyes of Katherine Maltwood, are manifestations of the *Caer Sidi,* the *Cauldron of Ceridwen,* the Zodiacal *Temple of the Stars.*

The previous reference to an early cosmopolitan civilization suggests immediately the possibility of Sumer as the true pre-historic cradle-land. The earliest literary reference to the Zodiac is in the *Gilgamesh Epic,* in the second millennium B.C.[4] Here the epic cycle is related to the solar cycle, the adventures of Gilgamesh,

Plate VII. Is this Camelot? An article containing a preliminary report of excavations appears in the Antiquaries Journal Vol. 47, 1967, 70–76. In this article, "A Reconnaissance Excavation at South Cadbury Castle, Somerset, 1966", by Leslie Alcock, there are photographs of some significant finds as well as an aerial view of the site. These excavations demonstrate the occupancy of the hill-top of Cadbury early in the third millennium B.C. which would agree with Mrs. Maltwood's dating for the Glastonbury Zodiac construction, but of course does not confirm it. (*Photograph by courtesy of Aerofilms*)

Plate VIII. The Chalice Well.

under the patronage of the sun god, as this is inscribed on twelve tablets. That is to say, on these tablets is recorded the story of the relation between the adventures of the hero to Venus (Ishtar), the Bull (Taurus), the Lion (Leo) and the episodes in the terrestrial life-cycle—"from the cradle to the grave"—in relation to the ceaseless cycles of the full moon and summer solstice, with the final downward plunge toward darkness and death (the waning moon and the dying sun). In a striking way this provides a prototype for Mrs. Maltwood's interpretation of the cycles of adventures of King Arthur's Knights as they journey through the circle of the effigies (celestial constellations). Perhaps it tends to support her theory of the Sumerian-Chaldean origin of the Somerset Zodiac.

Doubtless there is much misty nostalgia in the legends of the Zodiacal Holy Grailers. There certainly is something of the messianic theme at work, as we have seen. This is observed in the facility with which Arthur lends himself to the role of a Celtic Messiah. In some ways the "second coming of Arthur" resembles the "second coming of Christ." As time moves on and it becomes clear that the prophecy has not been fulfilled, the predicted event can easily be postponed into the more distant future. Meantime, if the hopes are dimmed, they do not die. There is a myth of social immortality at work here.

Thus, bathed in the dim religious light of medieval knighthood, Arthur of Camelot fades into the soft and wistful afterglow of the golden age—nevertheless always ready to ride forth once more and do battle in the cause of righteousness. Will Arthur be needed? Will he be ready, if needed? Here Merlin, the magician, is silent. The Sybils are inarticulate. The Glastonbury Zodiac reveals not the future, and the voices of the Abbey monks whisper only of the past—with one possible exception! Should the time come when Arthur does return to Avalon, those "of the faith" will echo the cry of the ancient initiates: *Christ is my Druid!*

From Indian *Asura*—Iranian *Ahura*—Egyptian *Osiris*—Palestinian *Christ*—British *Arthur*: this is the social transubstantiation inherent in the alchemy of magnetic moments in the spiral of time. Which of these is the "real" Arthur? Are they successive layers of the laminated image that grows with time? If so, how did all this get started? And how will it end?

III. THE THREE FACES OF ARTHUR

In this domain, where pre-history and prophecy are so closely interwoven, it is difficult to disentangle fact and fancy. My own best guess is that we are here dealing with three different but related "Arthurs"—the trinitarian doctrine of Arthur, one might say. Perhaps there are even more, further back in time. I do not know whether the Medean (Persian) god *Ahura* is a kind of prototype; but certainly the Assyrian god *Assur*, the Egyptian god *Osiris*, the *Ar-Thor* of the legendary Atlanteans, and the English *Arthur*, may all stem from the same prototype. Perhaps through the several masks of Arthur one may discern behind the Indo-Iranian god some still earlier Aryan god of the Indo-Europeans. Were the people who worshipped this primordial god in its earliest embodiment the creators of the Glastonbury Zodiac? In any event, this earliest god of the Zodiac of 5,000 years ago is the first hint we have of the Arthur theme—the first incarnation of Arthur, as it were.

The second Arthur is the son of the Zodiacal Arthur. This is King (or General) Arthur, he of the Knights of the Round Table. He arrives more than 3,000 years later, about 500-600 A.D. According to Mrs. Maltwood, the adventures of this king were modelled after the sequence of constellations in the celestial zodiac.

The third Arthur comes with the era of the troubadours of the age of chivalry, which further transformed the non-astrological Knights into the seekers after the "Holy Grail." This is the next incarnation of Arthur and the Arthurian theme. The role of Arthur III as the culture hero of Mallory's and Tennyson's "Round Table" stands in the same relation to Arthur II as the "Teacher of Righteousness" stands in relation to Jesus, the Christ. As in the case of Asura (or *Ahura Mazda?*), the identification or "personification" of the later Arthur was made after the death of the previous Arthur.

All this still allows the romanticists to argue—if they wish—that the builders of the Avalonian Zodiac were, or may have been, refugee Atlanteans, and it is they who provided the archetypal god-Image, and this figure then, in turn, became the second Arthur in England and/or the Zoroaster (of Mazdaism) in Iranian culture. This latter hypothesis, however, might require that we subscribe to the view that there were two Zoroasters (an idea already

64

put forth independently by some speculators), the earlier one separated in time by many centuries from the Historical Zoroaster of the sixth century B.C. (approximately).

This, too, permits our messianic millennialists to assert further that the purpose behind this epic drama is to work out humanity's predestined course: mankind periodically loses its way, and the only manner in which it can regain its bearings and course is to rediscover the plot (map) of this cinerama. But this plot is half-revealed and half-concealed and men must progressively decipher the meaning of the labyrinthine adventure. Today this calls for a vast interdisciplinary research into the symbolism of the Somerset saga. As in Dante's *Divine Comedy*, to save ourselves man must rediscover the structure of the universe and the giant effigies on the plain of Somerset is the plan of "heaven on earth." The more imaginative devotees will affirm that the constellations point to the Occident because it is there, from the ocean depths, that Atlantis will arise and surface—as Edgar Cayce predicted—and men will go forth to create the New Jerusalem of the West.

In line with this world-view, the romanticists, perhaps following Blavatsky, will point out that the British Isles, having survived the deluge of Atlantis, were destined to become the cradle of the English speaking peoples—the nations which have contributed so much to the colonization and education of the continents and thus have urged forward the spread of knowledge. There is an old prophecy which, it is said, lies hidden in the cryptic writings of Nostradamus, that Great Britain, after she lost her world leadership, would still retain leadership in spiritual truth. That is why England, Scotland, Iona, and Ireland are "sacred centers"—at least so say the students of the mysteries. Of course, if this is to come to pass, England will surely require a cultural transfiguration, and as of now this is not on the horizon.

IV. FIRE FROM GLASS

As we have noted several times previously, in one way or another "glass" is usually associated with King Arthur and Glastonbury (the fort of *Glaes*). But that glass should also emerge as a component of the Stonehenge mystery is quite surprising. And yet such

65

may be the case. At least this is the thesis of two students of the "Mysteries," Flavia Anderson and Blodwen Davies. Let us see what each has to say.

In her volume, *The Ancient Secret* (London, 1953), Flavia Anderson is interested in the fact that in the very early Celtic Church a crystal ball was used to light a candle at dawn. This "homeopathic magic" is part of a broader pattern which includes the Beltane fire festivals of the Celts, when all new fires had to be started by the king with a burning glass. Also involved in these cultural activities are the involvements of the serpent and a glass egg, the latter apparently being a rock crystal used as a burning glass. Today the term "crystal ball" is used scornfully as a synonym for phony prophecy, but once it played a genuine role in the initiation ceremonies in the Mysteries.

It may be that in an earlier epoch the discovery of crystal, abundant in the Alps, gave rise to the idea that it was petrified ice. Before the discovery of the art of glass making, this crystal was known as *glaes*. After the discovery of glass making, blown glass was made into spheres which could be sealed and thus substitute for rare crystals. Mrs. Anderson's theory is that these water-filled glass spheres were used in ceremonies at dawn at the solstice to focus rays of light to create a spark in prepared tinder on an altar. In support of her theory, Mrs. Anderson appeals to the fact that fires in laboratories have been started by glass spheres filled with liquids standing in the sunlight.

It is known that sacred fires are associated with the winter solstice, the zodiacal sign on the horizon at the time of Virgo (therefore the time of the birth of the sun god, "born of the virgin"). These glass spheres were a part of the Druid eggs which featured their rituals. Thus not only is Glastonbury a "place of glass" and a "fortress of light," but generally there was a religion of sun worship and a homeopathic magic of sun-glass-fire rituals and ceremonials.

So far as one can learn from this book, Mrs. Anderson does seem not to have any knowledge of Mrs. Maltwood's studies. True, at the time Mrs. Anderson wrote her book, there was less interest in and knowledge about the Glastonbury story. So it is up to later students to provide the synthesis, if there is to be such. This has been accomplished, in part at least, by Blodwen Davies. Let us glance at this.

For her foundation, Miss Davies goes back to Professor Hawkins's research on the meaning of Stonehenge as an astronomical computer. Here it is shown that the Stonehengers lived by the sun and the moon, and that the sun at the winter solstice rose over the heelstone of Stonehenge, as millions saw this impressive documentary on the television screen. So much for the heelstone. But no one has come forward with the reason for or purpose of the altar stone—not until Miss Davies proposed the theory that there was a burning glass and tinder on the altar stone. As she put it, "the tinder may have been a little pine tree, the Tree of Life. (One wonders: would the Druids have preferred the oak tree or the mistletoe?) Thus was the burning glass employed in the sacred ritual of Virgo.[5] While she does not say this, Miss Davies' idea could be extended to mean that the "Holy Grail" may have been nothing other than a glass sphere or lens for focusing light to build the fire of the ancient sun worshippers of Druidic and Celtic culture.

One cannot say at the moment how plausible this interesting theory may turn out to be. But in a way it fits in with my own theory of God as the Cosmic Lens, the glass lens or "egg" of the Druids being one example of the earthly embodiment of the Supreme Imagination. Thus the Cosmic Imagination functions as the mediator between the *Guiding Fields* of the unmanifest world and the *matter* of the sense-perceptible or manifest world.

The ancient formula, "God is Light," is still a part of the truth about the universe. But somehow we will need to work out the analogy between the radiant sun and the crystal of consciousness, the latter being a refraction or reflection of a sublimated or spiritual light focused through a "cup" which is the origin of the legend of the "Holy Grail" of an age-old tradition.

With these obscure Hermetic utterances we take leave of the historical aspects of the labyrinthine mystery-play—one of history's great magnetic moments. There still are some items of unfinished business, to be taken up in this next section. And following that, we must try to knit together the various strands of fact and fancy into some recognizable pattern of meaning.

V. UNFINISHED BUSINESS ON THE TOR

It is quite obvious from the preceding discussions that the problem of the verification of the existence of the Zodiac will be a matter of crucial importance. There are several possible forms of such confirmation. In the first place, if disciplined observers were able to bear witness and say of the mosaic, "there it is," and then agree upon the positions and outlines and identities of the effigies ("constellations"), this would go a long way toward an empirical verification of Katherine Maltwood's findings.

In the second place, if one can make deductions and look for, *and find*, the predicted facts, this would add to one's confidence in the validity of Mrs. Maltwood's reasoning. In this connection, the only

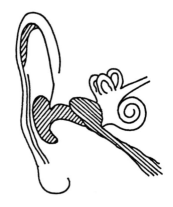

"Orion the Giant's" ear?

DUNDON BEACON on tip of Somerset. There is probably a passage way from the ear hole to the clearing!

Fig. 11.

deduction which Mrs. Maltwood made, with which I am familiar, has to do with an underground passage which she believed to exist, and which could be opened up by excavations. This passage, she surmised, would be found under the Giant's Ear—Orion's effigy. (see Figs. 11 and 12).

Apparently Mrs. Maltwood regarded this as quite important. In the "Bible Box" at the Maltwood Museum, Mrs. Mary E. Allan found an envelope marked on the outside, "important for excavation." Inside the envelope was a photo of the "Giant's Ear," outlined for excavation. This ear is sketched as the semicircular canals of the inner ear, and this presumably is the pathway to be excavated. In Fig 13 we have a reproduction of Mrs. Maltwood's free-hand drawing of Orion, and this corresponds to the airview, though it does not add anything to our information.

The reader may well wonder why there should be such a passage way. The best answer—perhaps the only one—is that Mrs. Maltwood believed that Glastonbury Tor was "England's Great Pyramid of Egypt," and like the original in Egypt was one of the world centers of the Mysteries. According to Mrs. Evelyn Swanepoel (who is my source of information at this point), the pattern of the center of the ancient mysteries was the same, that of a mound or a pyramid, with an inner chamber entered by an underground passageway. This is symbolic, of course, as well as a part of the actual construction. According to Mrs. Swanepoel, there are those who believe that the Chalice Well was the original entrance to the chamber within the Tor, leading to the Tor Hill chamber by this underground passage, which is now blocked by a fall of earth. The Chalice Well (see Plate IX) became a "well" by diversion of an underground spring of water, thus closing the entrance way to the Tor's inner chamber.

I am not presently in a position to assess the value of this line of thought. In response to my inquiry about a blocked passage, Professor Philip Rahtz has informed me that, "I did not find any subterranean passages on Glastonbury Tor." But his investigations are still incomplete, and what the future holds in store is still in the realm of the unknown.

Another item of unfinished business introduces a coincidence— that of an air-view of a second "ear." In a "close-up" examination of *Canis Major* one sees the "Great Hound" that guards the entrance to the "Kingdom of Logres" at Athelney. Our collaborator at this point, Mrs. Mary E. Allan, finds, in the "Bible Box," a note relative to this, as follows:

The Langport Somerset Wassail
"The girt Dog of Langport
he burnt his tail"

There follows a description of the Hound: *Head Drove and Head Rhyme are on his neck, below his mouth another Head Drove; to the west of his ear is Earlake, Moon's Drove lies in his mouth opposite to Athelbury where Alfred burned his cakes—Alfred's Fort. Burrow Wall, Athelney and Burrow Bridge outline his head, Parrett River the jaw. According to Wassail the dog is "girt"—fastened to what? Langport. He has a long tail. At night, Xmas, and New Year Wassail, "he burnt his long tail"—the festive drinking.* So says the "note."

Something of the symbolic significance of this—as she sees it—appears in another of Mrs. Caine's letters to me. She, too, recalls the wassail song in the Oxford *Book of Carols.* According to Mrs. Caine, the line, "The Girt Dog of Langport has burnt his long tail," means that Alfred was obviously an initiate into the Mysteries of Britain and in burning the cakes he was performing a mnemonic ritual act—as did Orpheus with the great guardian dog.

Mrs. Caine also finds significance in the fact that in this effigy are represented three early (prehistoric) settlements, forming a triangle, each point eleven miles apart from the other, within the Zodiac circle: Alfred Burrow on the dog's nostril as the southwestern point; the giant Tor as the northern; and Cadbury Castle or Camelot as the south-east. Strange triangulation! Stranger still—the dog's ear is at Earache Moor and his tail is at Wagg! What does this mean? Is there any significance to *place-names* in this mystery?

There is another item of unfinished business that must not be overlooked. This is the problem of whether Tor Hill is "natural" or "artificial." This is a question that has a bearing on some other matters, as we may note.

In the first place, if Tor Hill is natural, i.e., is *not* made by man, it is more difficult to suppose that there is a passageway under the Giant's "ear." Of course, such a passageway could have been dug out even in a natural hill—but this, like the spiral pathways (terraces) on the outside of the hill would be a difficult engineering feat.

According to Professor Philip Rahtz, the engineering technology required to put the plan of the ancient maze on Tor Hill—as according to Mr. Russell's theory—would *not* be impossible in the second

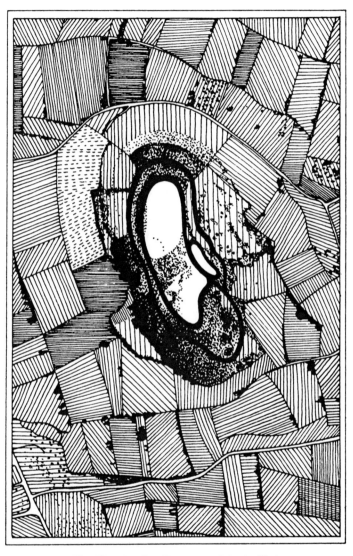

Fig. 12. Dundon Beacon as Orion's 'Ear'

71

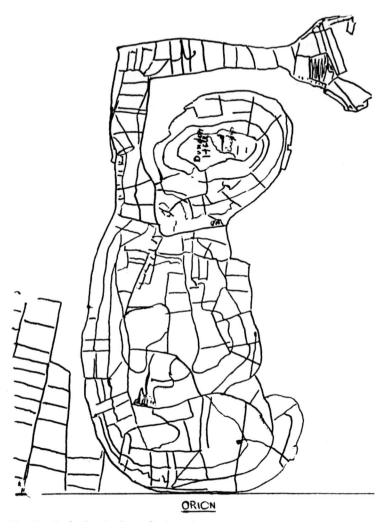

ORION

Fig. 13. Katherine Maltwood's line drawing of Orion. "There is probably a passage way from the ear hole to the clearing", she states

millennium B.C. If confirmed, this idea would be of value in helping to establish Glastonbury as a religious center long before Christian times. We know, of course, that at the present time there are workers digging over what must be the top of the inner chamber, if Mrs. Maltwood is correct in her thinking, so that if they dig deep enough, *they could cause the roof of the inner chamber to collapse*—as was the case with the Camster Mound in North Scotland, as Stuart Piggott explains in his volume on *Neolithic Culture in the British Isles*. If this same thing should happen on Tor Hill, Mrs. Maltwood would be vindicated.

In mulling this over, one must not overlook some rather far-fetched possibilities (seemingly so because of established "prejudices"), such as that Mrs. Maltwood's hypothecated "organ of Corti" of Orion's "ear" strikingly resembles the spiral patterns of New Grange, and elsewhere, perhaps because these all have a common cultural origin.

Our first assumption (above) is based on the supposition that the paths on and in Tor Hill (like the pyramids of Egypt and the ziggurats of Sumer) were put there as part of a total human construction job. The other possibility, of course, is that the hill is natural, i.e., created by recognized geological forces, so that the terraces or "paths" would then reflect the different rates of erosion, the harder strata being less subject to erosion and thus "standing out." In any case, what needs to be done next is to excavate the terraces and the hill and learn the true nature and the date of the formation of the hill. All this is part of the "unfinished business" on and in the Tor Hill. We have hardly begun.

VI. MAGNETIC RESONANCE IN HISTORY

The materials spread before us provide a banquet of strange assortment—myths, fairy-tales, legends, and history. We have here a mixture of archæological findings and metaphysical speculations such as may not be found anywhere else on this planet. As one reflects on this montage of fact and fancy, the thought comes to mind that the Glastonbury Tor is like Tennyson's "flower in the crannied wall"—if we could understand it, we would know what man and god is. As we have proceeded, the story has become "curiouser and curiouser," as Alice put it.

73

The task of formulating a unified theory admittedly is formidable. What the various strata of the saga have in common is a place, the Somerset area, a long and interrupted cultural background and history, and a psychological archetype inherent in a group of people within whom the "soul of Britain" is slowly emerging. Some would add to this the influence of an astrological zodiac which somehow focuses through the Tor like the sunshine through the trilithon of Stonehenge—a burning glass that has illuminated the area from the epoch of the Celts, and their predecessors, through Druid days to the time of King Arthur and the later monks of the Glastonbury Abbey.

The unquiet spirits of the Abbey monks, it is said, have some sort of message for us today, still undeciphered. In a whimsical mood, one might venture to suggest that the spirits of the monastery monks have established communication contacts with the more ancient spirits of the Druids and the messages which issue from their "combined operations" will confirm the archaic tradition that "he who goes through the Tor will reach Paradise"—the hidden meaning of this apparently being that *he who goes through the Mysteries of Initiation within the Tor will achieve illumination.*

Whatever one may say about all this, no one at the present time— it seems to me—is in a position to show convincingly that he has the final solutions to the major problems. To attempt to give the definitive answers to the "Mysteries of Britain" would be premature. Nevertheless, I shall propose a tentative theory in a moment. However, before advancing any hypotheses of my own, it is well to review some of the high spots of this saga in time and space.

Some Recurring Themes

What are the major "themes" of this time-spanning drama? And what are the presuppositions of others who have accepted the historicity of the several acts of the drama? This is really a question of the common assumptions made by those who are members of the "New Company of Avalon"—those who, rightly or wrongly, are dedicated to the task of vindicating Katherine Maltwood's findings and her astrological interpretations of these discoveries.

In the first place, it is clear that the "new Avalonians" (I use the term for convenience's sake) do not question the validity or reality (objectivity) of the effigies and their places in the Zodiac of Somerset. Others at the outset of their studies may want to raise

74

questions concerning the outlines of what one "sees"—whether they may not be partly or wholly imaginative. This, for them, would be the reason why there are such questions about "labyrinth" or "phoenix." But without dismissing the role of fancy, we must also keep in mind that the foregoing alternatives need not be mutually exclusive—both could be correct, as we have previously noted. But if both pictures are true (objectively real), the complete integration would call for a unification of two culture-patterns in one all-inclusive synthesis. This would certainly be a major undertaking.

A second fundamental assumption of the New Avalonians—and a recurring affirmation from H. P. B. on down—is the basic doctrine of the existence of a group of Masters who possess an ageless wisdom that is transmitted from generation to generation, century to century, by way of those select and secret societies that are sufficiently evolved to understand the Mysteries.

Thirdly, along with this belief in a group of Masters or Adepts, there is the doctrine of an ageless and timeless synthesis. This has just been indicated, but needs further explication.

Part of the doctrine has associated with it a belief in the concept of a unified and cosmopolitan civilization spread over Asia (India primarily), the Near East, and the Mediterranean countries, as far as Iberia, England, and Hibernia. This broad hypothesis could include the possibility of an integration with—or intercultural borrowings between—the Sumerian and Cretan civilizations, these in turn possibly derivatives of an earlier civilization of *Atlantis*.

If one were permitted to extend the boundaries of this wide-spread cosmopolitan civilization, in time as well as in space, so that it goes back not only into the prehistoric past but extends closer to the historic era of the ancient world, one could speculate about establishing connections with the Druids, the Pythagoreans, and the Essenes.

These ideas about a very early prehistoric universal culture will seem preposterous to the orthodox scientists. But this never bothers the members of the Arcane schools. According to one esotericist, the Essenes represent the spiritual core of the Western races, and they were not merely a Jewish sect in Palestine. The origin of this sect goes back many centuries before Christ. Their activities were widespread geographically, constituting a universal occult Brotherhood long before the center by the shores of the Dead Sea. This

75

Essene group was a school of prophecy, or "parapsychology," according to Dr. Charles Francis Potter.

If one were so minded, one could make a sustained effort to connect the foregoing with the Eleusian mysteries. Whether this would imply that we then move in the direction of those scholars, like Flavia Anderson and Blodwen Davies, who favor the Mysteries as resembling more the pre-Indo-European culture which emphasizes the female reverence (a Mother Goddess) as the giver of life, rather than the father-gods of the Indo-European religions, is an open question. So much by way of a seeming digression.

The foregoing comments concerning the Essenes and their mission are in harmony with the views of Professor John M. Allegro, Lecturer at Manchester University, translator of some of the Dead Sea Scrolls and author of an important volume on that subject. Professor Allegro has set forth the idea that the word "Essene" goes back thousands of years to a Sumerian word meaning "diviner," as well as "physician" and "magician." These Essenes, Allegro believes, had a secret knowledge of astrology and sought in the stars (zodiac?) signs that, for them, foretold the coming birth of the Christ child.

Obviously, this interpretation of Essenism as falling within the world of dark magic, particularly that kind which deals with the calling up of the spirits of the dead, is quite unorthodox—not at all congenial to customary Judaeo-Christian preconceptions. The views of Professor Allegro require a complete reinterpretation of the meaning and original purpose of the *New Testament*. Scholars must now look into these new claims and appraisals. My own views on the matter are set forth in the volume, *Cosmic Humanism* (Ch. X), some of which are relevant to the present discussion.

Finally, among the "New Company," we must note the tendency to elevate Great Britain to some peculiar and unique role in mankind's progress—a "once and future" thing. The tradition which made England a great nation in the past will be revitalized and transformed and Britain will once more lift the human spirit to new and higher levels. How the Glastonbury Zodiac, finally confirmed, supposedly could assist in restoring the ageless wisdom has already been indicated in previous pages.

So much for a recapitulation of the recurring major themes. We have neglected some of the minor themes—such as those of the "pyramidologists," because in the latter instance the ideas in this field are still too vague and tenuous to be integrated into our overall synthesis. To this, Mrs. Evelyn Swanepoel may not agree, and in the course of time she may be proven to be correct.[6]

What Mrs. Swanepoel affirms—as a devotee of Atlantean-Egyptian esotericism—is not beyond the bounds of the possible; but when, in addition, she supposes that the Atlantic bridge made it feasible for later migrants from Algeria to invade Aztec and Mayan civilizations, one becomes dubious. How can one test and confirm (or refute) such far-flung hypotheses?

But if the Arcane school of pyramidologists is correct and the British zodiac builders did in fact receive their astronomical and engineering know-how from the Egyptians, it will be necessary to move the era of the pyramid builder backward in time to a much earlier age, one that permits Egyptian culture to antedate the Somerset zodiac of 5,000 years ago. This requirement, however, would not disconcert our esotericists. I am told by Dane Rudhyar that the Bahai archæologist and Egyptologist Leon Getzinger insisted that the pyramids were built an entire precession-of-the-equinoxes cycle of 26,000 years before the date officially accepted today, the stars having returned to the same place at the end of the cycle. This unusual view is defended on the basis of alleged marine shell incrustations on the pyramids at a certain height above the sand level, indicating that the territory had been partly submerged at some time (or several times) by the sea.

This idea would fit in with the general surmise that there was some sort of Atlantic civilization which was transmitted through small groups of advanced ("divine") persons, some of whom were the rulers of very ancient Egypt—around 30,000 B.C.—when, according to the theory about the positions, orifices, and passageways, the Great Pyramid was built, i.e., a complete precessional cycle of 26,000 years.

If one were inclined to let his fancy roam at will, all this could be related to H.P.B.'s idea that the Americas and Eurasiafrica were formerly one continent which slowly drifted apart. While the subsequent disappearance of Atlantis may have occurred over a considerable period of time, the seed of the present humanity allegedly would have been formed about a million years ago, when, with the disappearance of Poseidonis, the Atlanteans could have moved

77

eastward to Eygpt and Britain and westward to the Americas. This (above) growing idea of an Atlantic land-bridge is quite in harmony with Wegner's theory of "drifting continents"—an idea now finding support in research on paleomagnetism and reversals of geophysical polarities. But whether the time scales are proper for all this wondrous metaphysical spiderweb of geophysics, archæology, anthropology, and human history is certainly open to question.

Some Soaring Speculations

For a complete theory of any complex social phenomenon one requires a full-blown philosophy of history and theory of man. In a subsequent volume, now in preparation, I shall attempt to present such a complete philosophy and purview. This will be a non-linear and wholistic interpretation. In that more complete statement two facets will receive further elaboration: (1) there will be an organismic theory of the earth as a living entity, with human society as a part of that evolving giant creature; and (2) there will be a theory of the origin of human consciousness in terms of its bi-polar sources in (1) the human nervous system, and (2) the radiation belt (or *psi*-field), the two poles, between them generating the "world sensorium" —the guiding field which controls the psychosocial evolution of mankind.

On the side of the earth-organism, we have long argued the case for the doctrine of the evolution of a giant earth-creature, the idea that the earth is indeed a living being, with the plant and animal kingdoms forming (functionally) the entoderm and the ectoderm of the giant earth-egg, with the human race constituting the maturing nervous system of the embryo and individual persons serving as the "neuroblasts" of the creature. We have urged that the eastern and western hemispheres are analogous to the right and left lobes of the human brain, together constituting the armature of an earth-dynamo spinning out the lines of force ("wires") of the coming electromagnetic society.

Accordingly, the planetary cortex of the electromagnetic society gives rise to its radiation-belt "electroencephalograms." These are the lines of force of the *psi*-field that are associated in cause-effect relations (feed-back) with the two halves of the earth-armature and the subordinate ganglia of the global cogitatorium. The evolving system of life is operated by the energy of the sun (as the ancient

Druids knew), which elaborates the essential substances (e.g., chlorophyll) that the earth-egg requires.

The human beings (neuroblasts) of the differentiating forebrain are not yet the perfect neurons they will later come to be. This, of course, implies that human history, the rise and fall of nations, the migrations of peoples, cultural diffusions, and the rest, are phases of the rhythmic pulsations of the planetary electroencephalograms, playing like electric signs over a bank of lights.

Magnetic Resonance in the Psychosphere

Clearly an important concept in this interpretation of history resides in the notion of consciousness which seems peculiar to the philosophy of a "cosmic humanism." This theory rejects the elementalistic notion of consciousness as something identical with events or activities in the human cortex, or more generally, the cerebral hemispheres. Putting aside the "inside the skull" or "under the hat" views of psychic experience, we hold that consciousness is a manifestation of a feed-back polarity between the human cortex and the environing "radiation belts" of a "world sensorium," this latter being our substitute for the *Noosphere* of Teilhard de Chardin. These postulated fields—or psi-belts—have their "magnetic moments" (perhaps there is only one psychic field).

The magnetic moments approach provides for the synchronicities between levels or planes of action-patterns, which are the secular-historical events occurring over the surface of the earth and reflecting a kind of electromagnetic induction. The field-aspects constitute the akashic records which provide the prototypes that may constitute the morphogenetic images in the various eras of human endeavor and achievement. Diagrams for these "thought forms," with places for the Yang-Yin motifs, are given in my book on *Cosmic Humanism*.

These sketchy suggestions concerning the manner in which the events of the matrix of history fit into the larger pattern of an emerging world sensorium need further clarification. But new ideas are becoming available. When all this conceptual equipment is harmoniously integrated into a rounded out explanatory system, we can get to the details. We will then have a more fully developed theory of the emergent levels of consciousness, and the place of intuition in human existence. This latter will not be merely a statement of the

79

role of "hunches" as rapid output of fragmentary bits of knowledge based on prior individual experiences, but a theory of intuition as prehensions of the coming-to-be-known. These insight-meanings or intuitions will appear as a result of (a) the ability to "scan" or "read" the information resident in the psychosphere (Noosphere), and (b) the ability to tune in on higher frequencies or forms of energy which are homomorphic with human levels.

Implicit in this philosophy will be a conception of the reasons for the constantly recurring themes in the various myths and legends among many peoples and cultures of the world. As we have seen, one constantly recurring theme centers around the pyramid or tower archetype. The Glastonbury Tor, which has been called "England's Great Pyramid of Egypt," was supposedly the center of the "Mys-teries." And whether the Tor Hill will eventually turn out to be the "Phoenix" or the "Labyrinth"—or neither, or both—the pattern, if it exists, is symbolic and serves to unite Heaven and Hell, God and Man. The Athenian watchers of the Tower of the Winds in the first century B.C. hoped thus to establish contact with their gods—a theme at least as old as the ziggurats of Sumer, the Tower of Babel, and the pyramids of Central and South America. Perhaps Schuré is right—there are two cosmic forces, one working centrifugally away from the earth and toward the sun, the planets, and the stars, and the other working centripetally, toward the earth.

In this respect the Jungian picture of the Grail as the reservoir of psychic energy is correct—the Grail is the focus of the com-muter or intermittent movement between the two poles within the psyche, sometimes called Heaven and Hell. Polarity rules the uni-verse—the polarity of North and South, East and West, Yang and Yin, centrifugal and centripetal, Heaven and Hell.

Finally, in addition to our need for some theory to explain the nature of the primordial wisdom religion with its mimesis of proto-typal culture patterns, it may be necessary to provide a scientific basis for reincarnation (metempsychosis). In connection with this latter, I am intrigued with the idea of the soul as a psychic energy circling the earth in a kind of super-physical magnetosphere, em-ploying here the notion of the duality of *phase*—versus *group*— velocities to explain why individuality within the wave-field does not slip off into astral spaces. This psychical sphericity is analogous to the manner in which radio waves are reflected back to and around the earth by the ionosphere. This deserves a fuller exposition, and that has been provided in my previous book, *Cosmic Humanism*. Here the idea of the *Psi*-field or *psychoplasma* is developed at some length.

What is the purpose of all this psychospheric apparatus? *What we need is a kind of eye in the sky for a kind of global vision of* earth-events. Here we have in mind the fact that the Glastonbury Zodiac and Stonehenge were constructed as if they were meant to be viewed from above—*precisely because in fact they were seen from above!* Here a resonance or configurational synchronicity between man's vision on the earth's surface and his purview by way of a planetary eye-brain hook-up is possible, provided the "lens" of the Cosmic Imagination is focused at the proper place at the right time (as is suggested in Fig. 14). At such moments of magnetic resonance symbols may appear on the screen of human consciousness and man's mind images a "clip" of a planetary cinerama—*as if an architect were looking into a heavenly mirror.*

In the distant past one great focal point for the Cosmic Lens, where rays forming a global image converged upon and met the magnetic field of a terrestrial humanism, was Palestinian Jerusalem. The Swedish seer, Emanuel Swedenborg, believed that he had a vision of the descent to earth of the "New Jerusalem," as this was prophesied in the New Testament book of *Revelation*. If, now, we are correct in our notion of Eastern Religion and Western Science as the two complementary lobes of the earth dynamo which in its rotation is spinning out a powerful current that supplies light and warmth and a guiding field for evolving humanity, then Glastonbury could serve as one more spot on this "Holiest Earth" as the place for this "Heavenly Pattern Upon the Earth"—to employ Mrs. Marjorie von Harten's[7] happy phrase. This time, however, the pattern is reincarnated in England and centered at the Glastonbury Zodiac. (as indicated in Fig. 15).

To complete this "social embryology" of world history—so briefly outlined here—much work remains to be done. Among other things, it will be necessary to strengthen the seemingly fanciful analogy between our proposed musical dissonance-to-consonance movement via the resolution of the "chords" of human history and the actual emergence of the *spherical harmonics* of the *planetary brain waves*. I intend this seriously and literally. This will have to

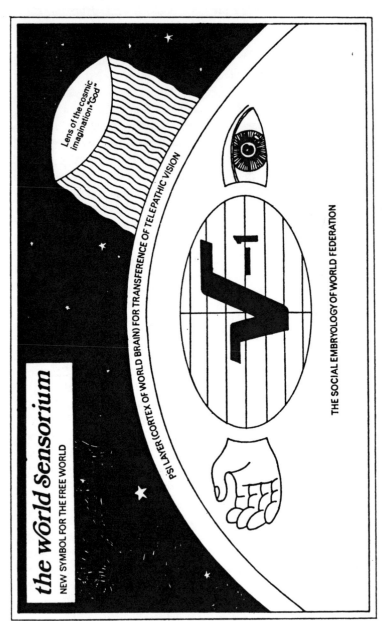

Fig. 14.

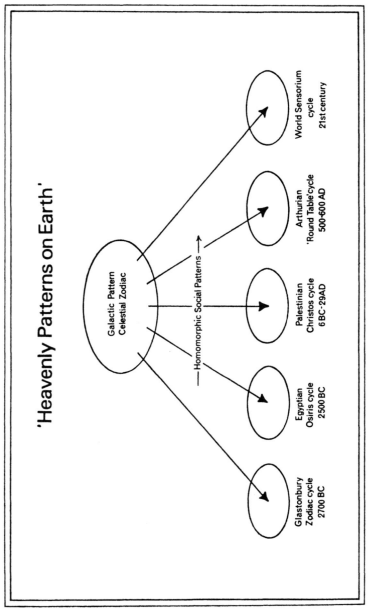

'Heavenly Patterns on Earth'

Galactic Pattern
Celestial Zodiac

──── Homomorphic Social Patterns ───→

Glastonbury
Zodiac cycle
2700 BC

Egyptian
Osiris cycle
2500 BC

Palestinian
Christos cycle
6 BC - 29 AD

Arthurian
'Round Table'cycle
500-600 AD

World Sensorium
cycle
21st century

Fig. 15.

be achieved by revealing the synchronicities between the *DNA* in the genetic units of the giant cell's "nucleus" and the *RNA* residing in the "cytoplasmic" envelope, which surrounds the cell, and the alternating current earth-fields, a concept now quite in harmony with the new knowledge of geophysics concerning the planet's *field reversals* over the eons. Our own vast parallelism requires that the "genes" correspond to the time-integrating musical patterns that express the monotonous vibrations that function as the "notes" or "letters" in the code of life, which is "social heredity." A somewhat similar analogy has been proposed by Preston Harold in his epoch-making volume, *The Shining Stranger* (1967, pages 106-109), and this needs to be integrated into the ongoing synthesis.

That this conception of a "spherical music" is not mere poetic license has already been demonstrated in the article, "The Music Logarithmic Spiral and World Unity," by Esther Watson Tipple and the present writer (*Darshana International*, India, Vol. V, 1965, 10-30). Further developments will appear in a forthcoming volume, *Magnetic Moments In Human History.* Any interested readers will have to exercise patience while this volume is being brought to completion. There the extraordinary possibilities for *Psi*-phenomena as they emerge in a "cosmic humanism" will be unfolded. In turn, to show how this will help us understand the pattern of the Zodiac mapped out on the "Holyest Erthe" of Glastonbury—this is part of the promissory note we have here pledged ourselves to redeem.

By way of conclusion, let us consider what some querulous critic may aver, namely, that I have here been guilty of a careless use of language. The fact is—the critic will assert—that primitive peoples built stone circles and spiral paths on tors in such a way that their gods, looking down from a higher dimension, would see man's handiwork and be grateful for this sign of adoration (as the primitives believed). But what you (Reiser) are saying is that the powers from on high helped man conceive and build the construction, as if in very truth the human architects were looking down through the eyes of their gods and in fact were inspired by (or in "resonance with") this higher visual cortex of the Cosmic Imagination. These, the critic urges, are two quite different interpretations—literal and figurative —*and which do you mean?*

The fact is that I am asserting *both* propositions—the *as if* and the *is*. This dual interpretation fits in with my earlier theory of the "bio-

84

logical origin of religion" via positive phototropism (heliotropism), where we seek to show that God is Light.[8] Man looks outward and upward toward his gods (or *Ahura Mazda*), and through the divinity he projects into the skies he, in his own imagination, looks down on his (man's) works and tries to see them as he envisions that his gods are seeing them. It is this inner-outer duality, the subjective striving to soar into union with the objective, which is the source of religions and man's "inner messiah." Here is the divinity in man which answers to the divinity in the cosmos—deep calling unto deep!

ADDENDUM

In June of this year (1968), and for the second time in two years, I visited the Maltwood Museum. I discovered that among the materials preserved by Mrs. Maltwood was a shallow wooden box containing some samples of earth and artefacts collected during the years of her research at the Zodiac site. One such was a package wrapped in a paper and marked on the outside with these words:

"The Lion's Tongue is made of red earth or stone.
Between Littleton and Compton Dundon."

I take it that this implied in Mrs. Maltwood's mind that the builders of the Zodiac had selected a red material for the Lion's tongue precisely in order to make it visible ("stand out"), especially if viewed from above (the sky). This is almost literally painting the "heavenly pattern" on the earth!

NOTES AND REFERENCES

1 Cf. "Building the World Sensorium," by O. L. Reiser, *Systematics,* Vol. 4, 1966, 42-58.
2 Cf. "Notes on the Somerset Zodiac," by Kara M. Pollitt, *Astrological Journal,* Vol. 9, (Winter, 1955-67), London.
3 Cf. "Points of the Compass," by Blodwen Davies, *Beacon,* May 1965, (page 90).
4 On the topic of the History of the Zodiac, see the volume, *Science and Culture,* by Noah Edward Fehl, 1965, Hong Kong.
5 This idea is set forth in her article, "Points of the Compass," by Blodwen Davies, *Beacon,* March 1966 (p. 247).
6 Cf. "The Great Pyramid," by Evelyn Swanepoel, *Beacon,* Vol. 42.
7 Cf. "A Heavenly Pattern Upon the Earth," by Marjorie von Harten, *Systematics,* Vol. 3, 1963, 1-18.
8 Cf. "The Biological Origins of Religion," by O. L. Reiser, *Psychoanalytic Review,* Vol. 19, 1932, 1-20.

Appendices

I. AT THE VICTORIA UNIVERSITY
MALTWOOD ART MUSEUM

Mrs. Maltwood's Bible Box. Contents of Large Cotton Folder as first checked by Mrs. Mary Allan, 1965.

1. Large and small Cardboards covered with important notes.

2. 1 Wrapper marked 'Air Survey Film and Prints and Star Charts —most precious'.

3. 1 envelope marked 'precious photos—Keep of Temple Area— Glaston'.

4. Brown paper folder marked 'Stars on Plates to fit map and Air Views of Zodiac—precious'.

5. Brown envelope marked 'Phillips Planisphere etc'.

6. In addition there is a second black folder embroidered containing Air Photos, which is inside the larger folder.
   There are also two of Mrs. Maltwood's books, namely 'Itinerary of the Somerset Giants with Maps' and 'King Arthur's Round Table of the Zodiac'.

The following note is attached to the outside of this cotton container:

"Discovery of the Signs of the Zodiac in Somerset, England, laid out on the ground near Glastonbury. This collection of maps and books must be kept safe. It will be of the greatest value some day. If anything is taken out of the black cotton case, it must be put back, because the collection is complete as it is. Most of the notes in the envelope can be burned if not wanted, but it would be best to seal up this old Bible Box with all its contents".

Contents of the Large Cotton Folder from Mrs. Maltwood's Bible Box checked by Mrs. Mary Allan and Mrs. Daisy Smith at the Museum, May 7th, 1968.

Packet No. 1. *Air Survey Film and Prints and Star Charts—Most precious.* Very fine photographs of King Arthur's Round Table—3 copies with notes by K.M. on back of one copy.
Tintagel. Newspaper picture of Tintagel—small old photograph of Zodiac, incomplete.
Photograph of Vase.
Envelope marked *"Precious photo—Keep of Temple Area—Glaston".*
* Copy of Country Life—January 11, 1946, illustrated article by Harwood Steele—Somerset Giants.
Note. See items 2 and 3 on 1965 List.
* Photograph of Mrs. Maltwood.
* Canadian and French Reviews of "A Guide to Glastonbury Temple of the Stars" 1. Hamilton Spectator Review. 2. The Land of the Sun, Review Etudes Traditionelles.
* Correspondence from Country Life—May 10, 1946, re: "Glastonbury Temple of the Stars".

Envelope No. 2. Brown cardboard Folder containing:
Air Survey—Mosaic Map.
Aries Air photo—Head and Foot turned backwards.
Two photographs — King Arthur's Round Table—five in all.
Bartholomews Map—England and Wales with attached Zodiac.
Two copies King Arthur's Round Table of the Stars.
The above corresponds to Brown Paper Folder, checked in May 1968. See item 4 on 1965 List.

No. 3. Phillips Planisphere of the Effigies—*most important proof.* See item 5 on 1965 List.

No. 4. Aerial photographs—Taurus and Orion by Aerofilms Limited, London, with notes on back by Mrs. Maltwood. 5, (all different) 2 of Orion (both different).

No. 5. Photographs of the Tor. Two Tor views. The Giant Orion. Photograph, The Giant Orion with film of photograph. Photograph of the Zodiac, taken from Mrs. Maltwood's model, by Dr. Pearce of Little Saanich Observatory. One photograph, possibly of Giant's Ear, cut to pieces, or of Dundas Beacon. Notes on back.

No. 6. Several photographs of Lion by Aerofilm Limited—all different with notes.

No. 7. Virgo and Scorpio—Photographs with notes on back of photos.

No. 8. Photographs of Aries with notes.
NOTE. Items marked * were not in the large Cotton Folder when first checked by Mrs. Allan, May 1965.

No. 9. Capricornus with notes.
Photographs in envelopes are not duplicates, but are views of various parts of each constellation.

No. 10. Tail of Dove. Photographs—notes on back of the Dove. Photograph Butleigh—with notes. 14 Hercules photographs—all different aspects— notes on back.
Note. No's 4 to 10 correspond with photographs in the large black silk embroidered Folder— checked in May 1965. In some of these envelopes there are parchment tracings of the complete constellations.

No. 11. Three photographs—2 Capricornus photographs —1 Nose of Aries—notes.

No. 12. *Large Cardboard.* This corresponds with item No. 1, as listed in May 1965. Typewritten on one side is Itinerary of the Zodiac, on the other is a map of Somerset, showing the Circle of the Zodiac around Glastonbury. The smaller cardboard of Mrs. Maltwood's notes has disappeared. Mrs. Allan drew attention to this fact, when she last checked the notes in October, 1967, and reported to Mr. Austin. A letter from Mr. Austin received subsequently, said the cardboard had been found and replaced. Mr. Fenger of the Island Blue print Company, has stated it was not in the Folder when he checked contents in January 1968.

Also in this Large Cotton Folder, there are two copies of Mrs. Maltwood's book, "Itinerary of Somerset Giants with Map."

Directions from Mrs. Maltwood attached to the outside of the Large Cotton Folder.

Contents of Large suitcase transferred from Mrs. Maltwood's Bible Box, which was checked by Mrs. Mary Allan, May 1965. These papers are now in suitcase, together with Large cotton Folder.

The following List gives contents of suitcase, checked by Mrs. Mary Allan and Mrs. Daisy Smith at the Museum, May 6th, 1968.

1. Orion's Ear—important for investigation if scientifically followed. This was originally in the large black cotton Folder, and we replaced it.

2. Letters in the Large suitcase, indicate the British Museum received copies of the "Enchantments of Britain" and photograph of Mosaic Map by Mrs. Maltwood—sent by John Maltwood in 1962.

Correspondence between John Maltwood and Miss Prior, Glastonbury, (Mrs. Maltwood's best friend) in regard to a copy of Mrs. Maltwood's Mosaic Map being retained at Glastonbury.

3. *Envelope marked "Precious".*
   Book on Druidism.

4. Survey of Zodiac—Hunting Aereo Survey Limited 1947.
   Various letters to Mrs. Maltwood regarding her work—*possibly of importance.*

5. Collection of interesting photographs from magazines bearing on archæological findings—Meare Lake Village—weaving combs and antlers and pottery.
   Advertising material featuring "The Meare Lake Village" by Arthur Bulleide, M.R.C.P., F.S.A. Antiquarian Society, and Harold St. George Gray, F.S.A., Assistant Secretary Librarian, Somerset Archæological Society, to be published under auspices of the Somerset Archæological and History Society.

6. Marked "Not important"—can be burned.

7. Marked "Can be destroyed"—cuttings on the subject of Glastonbury—packed envelope.

8. Zodiac—interesting notes—Roman villas in area—Arthur's Cave on Welsh border. Map showing Avalon—Reviews of "Temple of Stars." Edmund in "King Lear."

9. Important letters. Marked on outside of envelope: —
      St. George Gray
      Cranford and Hudson
      Bligh Bond
      Smith
      Dundun Beacon
      Watkins and Aerofilms
      Balch
      Steele

   True
   Willard
   Regan, etc.
   Lewis Spence
   Country Life
   Nuttall Smith
   Royal Society

10. Letters—Mrs. Maltwood to Penrose, also article from Country Life, January 14, 1949, by Harold Payne.

11. Clippings from various journals—also notes by Mrs. Maltwood on Signs of Zodiac in Kayser's Tympana.

12. All kinds of notes for use.

13. The Altar Table Legs at Somerton, Church of St. Michaels. Other clippings. Maps I-IV from Department of Astronomy, University of Toronto, Zodiacal Figures drawn by Mrs. Maltwood.

14. Marked—Interesting clippings. Marked—*Interesting and important.*

15. May 7, 1953. Various papers including article on King Arthur's Round Table and Zodiac.

16. Clippings and notes.

17. Letters and clippings.

18. Discovery of Nasca Figures.

19. The Wells Clock and other clippings.

20. Notes of much interest.

21. Correspondence with Miss Prior—Glastonbury.

22. Present day articles. Post cards and good Review.

23. Astrology Magazines.

24. King Arthur's Round Table and "Temple of the Stars".

25. Lewis Spence—An article on the Giants.
Mrs. Maltwood has written on the outside of most of these envelopes giving contents.
Book with illuminated cover contains clippings from magazines and newspaper Reviews of Mrs. Maltwood's work.
There are several copies of "The High History of the Holy Grail".
Eleven envelopes were not checked. These have been placed in two large manila envelopes, and marked.
There are parchment Rolls and Bundles of magazines and other books, etc.

II. THE PASSOVER PLOT AND CHRIST
AT GLASTONBURY

In his scholarly volume, *The Passover Plot* (Bantam Books, N.Y., 1967), Dr. Hugh J. Schonfield is concerned with the life of Jesus, especially the "silent years" of the childhood of the Messiah-to-be. The Gospels tell us little of this period. It seems strange that Dr. Schonfield as an Englishman is ignorant of (or more probably prefers to disregard) the British legend that Jesus sojourned in England during the time when his uncle, Joseph of Arimathea, was visiting this country. But let us suppose, what may not be the case, that Dr. Schonfield was familiar with this story, and after serious consideration had become convinced of its authenticity. In that circumstance, would not his reconstruction of the career of Jesus after his crucifixion have been altogether different?

According to Dr. Schonfield's picturization of the "Passover Plot," Jesus did not die on the cross. Schonfield points out (p. 156) that "it is by no means a novel theory that Jesus was not dead when taken from the cross, and some will have it that he subsequently recovered." This theme, he notes, was utilized by George Moore in his volume, *The Brook Kerith*, and by D. H. Lawrence in *The Man Who Died*. So, according to Schonfield, after Jesus apparently had expired—though in fact he was drugged to simulate death—his body was carried away by Joseph of Arimathea to a tomb (cave). Here Jesus recovered consciousness for a period, following which he died and was buried in an unknown grave in the vicinity. But Dr. Schonfield admits that the hypothesis that death came to Jesus *after* being carried from the cross is a theory that cannot be confirmed. According to Schonfield, after Joseph's task is fulfilled, "he completely disappears from New Testament records."

But if one treats seriously this attempted reconstruction, one might add further embellishments, for example, that after Jesus had recovered sufficiently from the wounds he suffered on the cross, he then—even though crippled in body—joined with Joseph on that famous journey to England, a journey which, as one Christian tradition in Somerset has it, transported also the Grail Cup to Glastonbury. A further extravaganza of theorizing might suggest that Mary, mother of Jesus, also was a member of the party that journeyed to Glastonbury. This, indeed, one legend records. If so, it would therefore be some sort of "poetic justice" that the saintly bones of the Virgin mother should lie under the crumbling walls of the Abbey, under the very remains of what had earlier been the wattle chapel, built perhaps by her own son Jesus.

One wonders: what conceivable purpose could have been served by any such miraculous configuration of events? And why should Jesus go to England a second time? What could he do there? And why do not the annals of history possess a record of this visit, with some reports of the subsequent life and deeds of the Messiah who, according to Christian theology, came to redeem the world? In that case, would not Glastonbury (England), rather than Rome, have become the center and focus of the new religion, rather than serve only as "Roma Secunda"?

While we are in this manner allowing our fancy to roam wide and free, might one not also wonder whether the boy builder of the "wattle church"—himself the son of a carpenter—may have toured the already pre-existent Glastonbury Tor, treading on the labyrinth (the "Grail," if Geoffrey Russell is correct), and perhaps even have entered the passage-way which, as Katherine Maltwood proposed, may have been the hidden initiation center of the "Mysteries." In that incredible circumstance the Holy Grail is but one facet of a multi-connotational symbol: it is not only the labyrinth on the Tor, but also the cup used by Christ at the last Supper, and perhaps even the chalice utilized by Joseph of Arimathea to catch the blood of Christ as he hung from the cross on the hill of execution!

As part of these far-ranging speculations, one might introduce at this point the allegory concerning the "chymical wedding of Christian Rosenkreutz," as this is recounted in the book, *A Commentary on the Chymical Wedding of Christian Rosenkreutz, Anno 1459,* by Margaret Bennell and Isabel Wyatt. (This document was presented to me by Mr. Geoffrey Russell.) Here we have the allegorical saga of Christian's voyage to the Tower of Olympus, located on an island which is square in shape (thus reminiscent of the *New* Jerusalem, which is also four-square), and here in the hidden laboratory of the Tower the work of the regeneration of man takes place. What is peculiarly interesting is the fact that the Tower (Tor?) has a ground-plan of seven interlacing circles—the plan of the ancient mystery temples—and it "stands seven storeys high," this of course being symbolic of the sevenfold nature of man. (Quite naturally, Mr. Russell underlined the "seven interlacing circles . . .," because for him the Tor circles are simply the paths of the Cretan labyrinth or maze.) If, however, Mt. Olympus, in the allegory, is situated in the "sea of the etheric," and not literally in the Greek peninsula, this then makes contact *with* Anwen and the astral world of the departed spirits (as mentioned earlier in the text), and this is in consonance with one symbolic meaning of the Tor of Avalon and the final "passover" of King Arthur.

If we are thus permitted to conjecture that Jesus did journey to England with Joseph, there to play some as-yet-not-understood and still-incomplete drama, one could conjure up a "plot" far more wondrous than that which Dr. Schonfield has been able to concoct. Recalling that King Arthur supposedly was descended of St. Joseph, *the Zodiac of Glastonbury then becomes a kind of antecedently designed creche for the birthing of the cycle of the Arthurian Knights of the Round Table—the "heavenly pattern of earth."* And then, perhaps, the quest for the Holy Grail on this "most sacred spot of England" (Avalon and Camelot) in turn becomes the prelude to the next act of this planetary mystery play. The final act of this apocalyptic drama lies ahead of us, in the unborn future. If so, one must venture, the Jews of Israel must somehow make their entrance upon the stage and play out their role in the incomplete pageantry of world history. If this be the case, do we have here the ingredients for a psychosocial alchemy, a religious renascence of world-wide import? In any event, willingly or not, the British Government, through the Balfour Declaration, *did* provide the Jews with a "Homeland"— *Israel.* But what will be the denouement of that?

In connection with the possible religious regeneration in England, and a subsequent global religious unification, it is interesting to note that the British are increasingly engrossed in their own historic panorama. One evidence of this is provided by the article, "Did Christ Come to Britain?," by Brendan Lehane (*Weekend Telegraph*, Dec. 16, 1966).

And now, in summary, what shall we say about the above marvelous embroidery on the "Passover Plot"? I believe that Mrs. Maltwood would reject immediately this embellishment, because, in the first place, she could not accept the idea that Jesus plotted his own crucifixion and "resurrection." This leaves untouched, however, the homology of the Celestial Zodiac and the "heavenly pattern upon the earth."

And for my part, I cannot regard Dr. Schonfield's reconstruction of the role of Jesus in a messianic conspiracy as plausible in the least. In my own approach to this broad and difficult problem, I prefer the interpretation that is set forth in my book, *Cosmic Humanism* (Chapter X). But whatever the final judgment on the "Plot" may be, the Glastonbury epic is still before us as an enduring challenge —whether Jesus visited it once, or twice, or not at all.

III. THE GLASTONBURY ZODIAC, PSYCHICAL POWERS, AND GEOMAGNETIC FIELD REVERSALS

For several years I have been doing research on the Glastonbury "Zodiac," this latter, according to Mrs. Katherine Maltwood, being laid out about 2,800 B.C. on the terrain of Somerset as a kind of "heavenly pattern on earth." If her claims are confirmed, this will constitute a more dramatic episode in the history of science and religion than Professor Gerald Hawkins' verification of Stonehenge as an astronomical observatory and computer. Assuming for the moment that such verification of Mrs. Maltwood's findings and claims will in time be forthcoming, a number of fascinating but nagging problems will arise and beg for answers. Among them are the following.

The architects and builders of this enormous Zodiac (30 miles in circumference) must have had a superb knowledge of astronomy and great engineering skills. But where did they derive this advanced knowledge of science and technology? Where did the Zodiac designers themselves originate? What happened to this civilization and its people, who could construct the "effigies" of a terrestrial zodiac but could not preserve themselves? Did the people who built this marvelous "teaching machine"—architects, astrologers, and engineers—disappear suddenly? Were the builders wiped out by some sort of disaster?

95

My own interest in these problems received added impetus as a result of increasing familiarity with the views of Miss Elizabeth Leader, a member of the "London group" interested in the Zodiac, Tor Hill (this latter being the Cretan labyrinth, according to Geoffrey Russell), Silbury Hill, and King Arthur's *Round Table* at Camelot —all in the same general area of West England.

Miss Leader's theory of what happened is based on the notion of the near approach to the earth of some extra-terrestrial body which introduced some alien radiation in the atmosphere with a corresponding disruption of life and disequilibrium of mental and physical balance. Her specific suggestion is that there was a connection between the pineal gland (chakra) which flames from the top of the head ("the knob and stalk of the Greek and Etruscan Griffon being not a bad picture of this gland and its fibres") and the loss to man of certain powers, this being analogous to man's expulsion from the state of Eden. Here Miss Leader appeals also to the Greek myth of Phaeton and similar stories which indicate that at some time in the past man enjoyed a state of simple living and high attainments, all of which were wiped out by some catastrophe in which the pineal gland was "sealed off" and the paranormal powers due to it were lost.

Miss Leader proposes that some body from outer space had rushed through the solar system "at a time when the planets were in line" (why is *that* necessary?) and had come so close to the earth that as it passed over the region of the Atlantic ocean it caused, first, a great cold, due to the obscuring of the sun's rays by clouds of dust in its train, and next an intense heat—white hot debris falling through the atmosphere. This, according to Miss Leader, could have been the cause of the mental-physical imbalance that explains the loss of powers and skills of the Zodiac builders.

In connection with this ingenious theory one must note that it is reminiscent of Velikovsky's supposedly "discredited" speculation about "foreign visitors"—but a theory which, curiously enough, is now being revived in the more "respectable" guise of the notion of an earth-comet collision, as the discovery of tektites brought up from the ocean bottoms has been interpreted to imply. This in turn is linked with the evidence for a reversal of the earth's dipole field some 700,000 years ago. I shall return to this field-reversal concept in a moment.

In passing one should also note that a theory of the "loss of powers" similar to Miss Leader's was advanced by Eleanor Merry in her volume, *The Flaming Door*, where (p. 41) she speculates that clairvoyance was a universal faculty in ancient times, "which depended upon a peculiar vibratory relation between two parts of the brain, whose functions, today, have become more or less atrophied as far as clairvoyance is concerned."

At the moment I am not so much interested in deciding who may be closer to the truth in the matter of the *physiological* basis of clairvoyance (i.e., "cerebral resonance," as I would call it, vs. pineal-chakra function) as I am in calling attention to another possible external (geophysical) cause for the loss of the clairvoyant function (the air-view vision) which the builders of the terrestrial Zodiac may have suffered. This latter suggestion is built around the new discoveries concerning the field-reversals revealed by paleomagnetism and studies of earth-polarity changes.

It is known that the earth's magnetic field undergoes cycles of weakening and strengthening as well as reversals of polarity.[1] The cause of geomagnetism is due either (1) to the constituents of the earth's iron-and-nickel molten core, which, as they rise to the surface, acts like the electrical conductors of a dynamo; or (2) in the novel theory based on the precession of the earth, every 28,000 years, where the resulting "precessional torque" provides the force which drives the earth-dynamo. The mounting evidences for field reversals, polar wanderings, and continental drifts are based in part on paleomagnetism (studies of the reversing of polarities of strata of ancient rocks which, when in the earlier molten state, are magnetized in the direction of the earth's fields). These polarizations constitute a "magnetic memory," as if they were compass needles frozen into the geologic strata. These field reversals have occurred nine times at least.

The evidence for these interlocking phenomena is good. At irregular intervals, ranging from 30,000 years to more than 2 million years, the polarity of the earth's magnetic field "flips over." Most importantly, this new theory of the dynamic earth has tended to revive and fortify Alfred Wegner's rehabilitated conception of the "drifting continents." It is now conjectured that as recently as 120 million years ago Africa, India, and the Americas were a single land mass, a gigantic island in a world ocean. In any case, the general theory

97

of the surface of the earth as a flexible and dynamic thing could have a bearing on the problem of the "Lost Continent of Atlantis," whether this be in the form as embraced by Professor Angelos Galanopoulos and John G. Bennett or in the original form as given in Plato's famous version. The elaboration of that theme cannot be undertaken here.

For us at this time, the more interesting consequence of the foregoing lines of investigation relates to the possible biological and psychological implications of field reversals. According to Dr. Robert J. Uffen, the reversal of the earth's field has casual effects in biology, for at the points in time when the earth's magnetism disappears the earth loses its shielding umbrella against the intense cosmic rays from outer space, and with the increasing dosages of radiation the mutation rate is speeded up. Perhaps it is appropriate to point out that this is in harmony with my own earlier guess concerning "Cosmecology" (Cf. "Cosmecology: A Theory of Evolution," *Journal of Heredity*, Vol. 28, 1937, 367-371), where it is proposed that the rhythms of mutation caused by cosmic rays are regulated by the sun as the "pacemaker of evolution" on the earth, and that this in turn reflects the dynamics of the solar system as a whole and perhaps even the entire Milky Way galaxy (on this point see Dr. Robert J. Uffen's comments on my theory as these are reproduced in my volume, *Cosmic Humanism*, 1966, pp. 440-441).

We previously mentioned the "far-out" ideas of Dr. Immanuel Velikovsky. One of the interesting suggestions in this area is the proposal that reversals of geomagnetic polarity may in some cases have been the result of extra-terrestrial intrusions, as Hoerbiger and Velikovsky have surmised. The cosmic bodies that strike the earth leave the evidence of the collision in the form of tektites. The accompanying "vanishing act" of the earth's umbrella, which protects living forms from the extra heavy doses of radiation from outer space, could in turn be responsible for the accelerated rate of biological mutations, with the disappearance of some old forms of life and the appearance of some new species (Cf. "Tektites and Geomagnetic Reversals," by Billy P. Glass and Bruce C. Heezen, *Scientific American*, Vol. 217, 1967, 33-38).

According to some scientists, tektites were deposited 700,000 years ago in the Far East, 35 million years ago in America and Libya, and 15 million years ago in Czechoslovakia. It has been calculated that, on the average, these geomagnetic reversals occur every 5 to 10 million years, but the rate has been accelerating with the passage of time. Currently the earth's field is decreasing in strength, and—as Dr. Bruce Heezen has pointed out—if this continues at the present rate, another reversal may occur in the next one thousand years—excluding, of course, other extra-terrestrial visitors, I would add. In any case, *the next reversal could soon be upon us.*

The amazing thing is that there is now evidence suggesting that the study of the galactic magnetism in a nearby spiral galaxy enables us to make conjectures concerning the polarity of the magnetic field of our own Milky Way galaxy. In studying the direction of the magnetic field lines in our own spiral galaxy, it turns out that the polarity of some parts of our galaxy's magnetic field is the reverse of that of other segments, and that these reversals occur systematically with galactic longitude, i.e., the polarity seems to be reversed at the plane of the galactic disk. To what extent it may be possible in thinking to pass from the earth to the galaxy, and back again, is an intriguing question. And is this "reversal" connected in any way with the twelve signs of the zodiac, i.e., the plane of the configurations which lie along the plane of the ecliptic? In one way or another, the macrocosm-microcosm analogy simply will not down!

If, indeed, these galactic reversals have some periodicity effect in their influences on the generation or/and emission of cosmic rays (especially if the galaxy is a cosmotron or cosmic ray generator) this would certainly support the "Cosmecology" hypothesis of a tie-in between planetary, solar, and galactic events as interlocking causal influences in biological evolution.

Now one wonders: what will be the biological and psychological consequences of the next disappearance of the "protective umbrella"? Will there be a new mutation in the human species—the "new humanity"? Or a return to an earlier and unified man, *Homo Atlanticus,* with the paranormal powers of the Initiates? *Cosmic Man redivivus?*

Such a conception would be quite consistent with Miss Leader's explanation, except that we have introduced also a field reversal related to excessive radiation, and this is what produced the physical imbalance (cortical-pineal dissonance) which she suggests as the basis for the loss of paranormal psychic faculties. To develop this further, let me now bring in some ideas from my former colleague-in-ideas, Miss Blodwen Davies (deceased September, 1966).

According to this student of esotericism, the meaning of higher initiation lies in the fact that at a certain degree the individual is no longer subject to the pull of the earth's gravity and can rise at will. Such Initiates could have planned the Somerset Zodiac, moving in space and time to design, construct, and *oversee* the Temple. Thus, without benefit of airplanes, they had the overview necessary to mark out and execute the design of the "effigies" of the Temple of the Stars. Perhaps they were refugee Atlanteans, the ship in the Zodiac being the symbol of their means of transportation to Glastonbury, the "land of the Logres." If so, we have here an Atlantean "scripture" of the evolution of consciousness—a "teaching machine" of planetary import—indeed, *the first World University!*

Now for some extrapolations of my own: I surmise that we will not discover the "meaning of the Zodiac" until we recover the superconsciousness of the Builders, and here the embryogenesis of the World Sensorium must lead the way. Or to put the matter otherwise: as we progress in the vast interdisciplinary process of revealing and understanding the message of the Zodiac, *we will reconstitute in ourselves the now-lost higher consciousness of those who built the Zodiac.* This is the planetary meaning of the Temple of the Stars, the "heavenly pattern on earth." This, too, is entirely consonant with the thesis of the Unknown Author of *The Shining Stranger* (1967), a work so heroically salvaged for us by Winifred Babcock.

Here, in summary form, are some of the major problems which confront those of us who are attempting to elaborate a complete philosophy on the basis of the Glastonbury Zodiac:

1) Is there any deep causal connection ("synchronicity") between geomagnetism, field polarity reversals, and the migrations of continents, as according to Wegner's hypothesis of drifting continents?

2) Does the "Double Helix" of geophysical and biological sequences require a synchronicity between the magnetoplasm and the sun's radiation, via the "solar wind," so that the sun is indeed the pacemaker of biological and psychic evolution, this in turn reflecting the overlordship of a wholistic or gestalt

solar system dynamics? Does this perhaps also require the co-operation of the entire Milky Way galaxy as our solar system revolves around the galactic center of our spiral galaxy (in the region of the constellation Sagittarius?)? In that case, there is some sort of resonance between the sun-system and the galactic magnetohydrodynamics.

3) Does the idea of a resonance between the two cerebral hemispheres as a basis for clairvoyance in man require that, on another level, the progressive history of the earth is correlated with the predestined separation of the proto-continent into two hemispheres, the Eastern and Western halves then becoming in fact the brain lobes of the earth-armature as the globe spins out the electromagnetic lines of force of an emerging *World Sensorium*?

4) Does the coming reunification of human consciousness via the coming mutant personalities depend upon the embryogenesis of a giant world organism, with each human being serving as a nerve cell (neuroblast) in the emerging synthesis?

5) Where and what is the "missing link" that connects the *DNA* double helix of the gene with the archetypal patterns which are resident in the *Psi*-field so that the "Cosmic Lens" can "twist the tail" of the *DNA* genetic units and guide the course of biological evolution? What "hazards" are involved?

6) What and where is the master timing device (the sun-planet-galaxy clock) which regulates the interdependent causal sequences to achieve and maintain the astro-geo-bio-homo-social chain of a vast, interlocking, and awesome teleology?[2]

These are not only my problems. Mr. John Bennett has indicated that he is formulating a tentative hypothesis that an esoteric school may have existed in Glastonbury prior to the destruction of Atlantis in 1450 B.C., and that this school may have left a permanent message in the form of earth signs ("effigies"). If the astronomers can come up with the necessary correlations and identify the group of aligned menhirs around Glastonbury Tor as having astronomical orientations at the various epochs at which the work was done, we will have evidence that there is an intelligence that works on a much larger scale than that of ordinary human experience. Here Mr. Bennett and I can agree. In any case, there are more than enough problems to go around.

[1]For a discussion of geophysical reversals of the magnetic field, see the following articles: "Reversals of the Earth's Magnetic Field," by Allan Cox, Richard Doel, and G. Brent Dalrymple, *Science*, Vol. 144, 1964, 1537-1543; "Paleomagnetism," by John Verhagen, *Science*, Vol. 147, 1965, 1069-1071; "Motions of the Earth's Core and Variations of the Main Geomagnetic Field," by Raymond Hide, *Science*, Vol. 157, 1967, 55-56; "Precession of the Earth as a Cause of Geomagnetism," by W. V. R. Malkus, *Science*, Vol. 160, 1968, 259-264.

[2]For a summary of the new knowledge about the magnetoplasm, see the following: "The Magnetopause: A New Frontier in Space," by C. O. Hines, *Science*, Vol. 141, 1963, 130-136; "Magnetic Fields in Interplanetary Space," by L. J. Cohill, Jr., *Science*, Vol. 147, 1965, 991-1000; and, "The Magnetosphere," by L. J. Cohill, Jr., *Scientific American*, Vol. 212, 1965 (March).

IV.   RECENT DEVELOPMENTS IN ATLANTOLOGY

Since the manuscript of this book was completed, four newly published studies have appeared bearing on the topics considered. A word about each of these will bring our own presentation strictly up-to-date. The first two books and the last two deal with similar approaches and subject matter.

The first volume is the valuable study by Professor William W. Kenawell, *The Quest of Glastonbury* (New York, 1965). This is a biographical account of Frederick Bligh Bond and his "psychic researches" into the historical realities of Glastonbury Abbey. In considering the purpose of this book the impression develops that the intention of Professor Kenawell's survey is to lead the reader in the direction of believing in the ultimate vindication of Bond's life-work. Professor Kenawell informs me that he has in his possession boxes filled with Bond's "verbal cryptographs" with numerical clues which he (Kenawell) has not yet deciphered. But whether these gematria may eventually be found to confirm or imply the validity of Mrs. Maltwood's claims cannot be determined at the present time.

Another book dealing with application of psychical research in the field of historical and archæological data is the volume by Hans Holzer, *Windows To The Past, Exploring History Through ESP*

(New York, 1969). Mr. Holzer's Chapter Five has the title, "Will the Real Camelot Please Speak Up! " It deals with the events supposedly taking place in the Glastonbury and Camelot areas.

Using his redoubtable medium, Sybil Leek, Holzer believes that they—between them—succeed in establishing contact with spirits on the "other side" and confirming that Cadbury Hill, overlooking the plains to Glastonbury, is indeed fabled Camelot. The claims of Bond concerning his Glastonbury Abbey research presumably also are indirectly strengthened.

Strangest of all, one voice that comes through Sybil's "entranced lips" turns out to be that of "Merlin" (so it is stated), counselor of Arthur, who gave forth a prophecy concerning a bird *Erfin*, to come forth from the earth and play a role in a "war that is yet to come." This, supposedly, is W. W. III. And Holzer then adds, "so much of this part of the world is yet underground, awaiting the spade of the archæologist."

But in neither of these volumes is there any mention of Katherine Maltwood and her investigations into the Glastonbury Zodiac. A strange oversight.

A third book, recently published, dealing with matters discussed in the present book is the volume by Patrick Crampton, *Stonehenge of the Kings* (New York, 1968). This book is of interest to us because, among other things, the author casts doubt upon Gerald Hawkins' theory of Stonehenge as a "Computer for astroarchæology." Mr. Crampton's alternative theory of the "Kings" (of a people from the East), who built Stonehenge, is that they were not constructing a pagan religious center or an astronomical observatory, but a fortress. The thesis is presented in a fascinating manner. I do not know what Professor Hawkins would say in rebuttal to the charge that he (Hawkins) is guilty of errors in the alignment of stones, a disregard for earth erosions over millennia, and other selectivities in handling data, which allegedly contribute to the development of his glamorous but fanciful theory.

For my part this is still an open question. If I were to indulge in wishful thinking, it would be to hope that someday there will be uncovered the firm evidences of a higher culture that supplied the inspiration, architectural design, and the engineering technology for the construction of the Glastonbury Zodiac, Avebury, and Stonehenge. This, I would judge, is closer to Hawkins than to Crampton.

Finally, the book by James W. Mavor, Jr., *Voyage to Atlantis* (New York, 1969) is important for our studies, because it makes out a strong case for the Galanopoulos-Mavor-Bennett thesis that Plato's "Atlantis" was really the Island of Thera in the eastern Mediterranean archipelago (including Santorini). Like Crampton's work, it attempts, negatively, to "de-mythologize" romanticist history, while positively seeking to confirm an alternative hypothesis. But if this thesis turns out to be correct, this does not upset any of my own views as tentatively set forth in this book. We are not necessarily committed to the Donnelly-Blavatsky-Cayce version of "Atlantis." But if, in a mischievous spirit, one were to try to kill two birds with one stone—both Crampton and Mavor—one might propose that there were in fact two Atlantises, one in the eastern Mediterranean and the other "beyond the pillars of Hercules." Then it would still be possible to hold that the "refugee Atlanteans" from the West could have built the Zodiac. And it would also be possible to argue that the builders came from the East. This would involve the utterly fantastic supposition that two peoples came together— from the East and the West—and met in England to undertake a common job. I know of one person who did entertain this "incredible" idea.

There is only one other piece I can supply for this puzzle picture. In her remarkable volume, *The Wine Dark Sea* (Chicago, 1964), the author, Henriette Mertz, refers (p. 89) to "Plato's familiar account in the *Timaeus,* of a large area of weeds in the sea, beyond the Pillars (of Hercules) . . ." This sea of weeds, according to the author, was the Sargasso Sea, which the Phoenicians of the third millennia B.C. had discovered. This sidelight seems to suggest that when Plato locates *Atlantis* beyond the Pillars of Hercules, and mentions also the Sargasso sea of weeds, he was not thinking of *Atlantis* in the eastern Mediterranean Sea. Indeed, there are those who believe that the weeds that cover great patches of water also are covering an ancient submerged land mass. And this, they point out, is not far from the sunken and soon-to-rise *Atlantis* of Edgar Cayce!

As time passes, it becomes quite certain that far back in the earth's history, Europe, Africa, and the Americas once formed a single mass—called "Gondwanaland" in contemporary geology— which subsequently broke up into separate continents, leaving only the mountainous ridge in the mid-Atlantic floor as a residue. A fanciful speculator might then conjecture that Plato's *Poseidonis*—somewhere near the Bahamas, or the Azores, or under the Sargasso Sea —was the last fragment of the collapse of Gondwanaland. But in terms of present knowledge such a possibility cannot be very helpful to those who want the "Atlantean refugees" to be the builders of the Glastonbury Zodiac. Certainly the break-up of the proto-continent is too far back in time for any such solution. At that time even "primitive man" had not yet arrived on earth. In general we must conclude that man does not yet know enough about himself and the planet earth, *This Holyest Erthe*, to formulate final conclusions.

Selected Bibliography

Adamnan, Saint. *The Life of Saint Columba*; translated by Wentworth Huyshe; first ed., London, 1905.

Anderson, Flavia. *The Ancient Secret*; London, 1953.

Ashe, Geoffrey. *King Arthur's Avalon*; sec. ed., London, 1963.

Blavatsky, H. P. *The Secret Doctrine (The Synthesis of Science, Religion and Philosophy)*; Adyar, India, 1888; London, 1928.

Bond, Frederick Bligh. *The Gate of Remembrance* (sec. ed.), Oxford, 1918.

————. *The Hill of Vision*, London, 1919.

Broderick, Alan H. *Father of Prehistory (The Abbé Henri Breuil)*; New York, 1963.

Childe, V. Gordon. *The Dawn of European Civilization*; London, 1957.

Clark, C. and Piggott S. *Prehistoric Societies;* New York, 1965.

Davidson, D. and Aldersmith, H. *The Great Pyramid, its divine message;* London, 1929.

de Camp, L. S. and C. C. *Ancient Ruins and Archæology*; New York, 1964.

Donnelly, Ignatius. *Atlantis: The Antediluvian World;* rev. ed.; New York, 1949.

Elder, Isabel Hill. *Celt, Druid, and Culdee;* London, 1962.

Evans, Sebastian (ed. and trans.). *The High History of the Holy Graal*; 1910.

Frazer, James. *The Golden Bough*; 1936.

Gordon, Cyrus. *The Ancient Near East*; New York, 1965.

Hawkins, Gerald S. *Stonehenge Decoded;* New York, 1965.

Homet, Marcel F. *Sons of the Sun;* London, 1963.

Insole, A. V. *Immortal Britain;* London, 1952.

Kramer, Samuel Noah. *Sumerian Mythology;* New York, 1961.

Lewis, Lionel S. *St. Joseph of Arimathea at Glastonbury;* London, 1964.

Mallory, Sir Thomas. *Morte d' Arthur*; London, 1919.

Maltwood, Katherine E. *A Guide to Glastonbury's Temple of the Stars*; rev. ed., London, 1950.

————. *Itinerary of 'The Somerset Giants'*; Victoria; B.C., Canada, 1946.

————. *The Enchantments of Britain*, Victoria, B.C.; Canada, 1944.

Merry, Eleanor. *The Flaming Door*; rev. ed.; London, 1962.

ÓRiordáin, S. P. and Daniel, G. *New Grange;* New York, 1964.

Reiser, O. L. *Cosmic Humanism*; Cambridge, Mass., 1966.

Spence, Lewis. *The Mysteries of Britain;* London (no date).

Teilhard de Chardin, Pierre. *The Phenomenon of Man;* New York, 1959.

Trench, Brinsley le Poer. *Men Among Mankind*; London, 1962.

Various Authors. *Michael, Prince of Heaven*; London, 1951.

Waite, A. E. *The Hidden Church of the Holy Grail;* 1909.

Woolley, Sir Leonard. *The Forgotten Kingdom*; Middlesex, England, 1953.

Lightning Source UK Ltd.
Milton Keynes UK
28 January 2011

166546UK00001B/165/P